T0008406

Praise for *Overflowing Mercies*

As a dad, I am starving for creative ways to gather my family around Scripture. *Overflowing Mercies* is an absolute answer to a frustrated prayer. The heart of God beats HARD in these pages. The reflections really get everybody chiming in, and the prayers might be my favorite part. We feel like we're praying with the Coopers! Craig, thank you for placing our hands in the hands of Jesus with your words. "How you write like that?"

WALKER AND LANEY HAYES, Grammy-nominated singer/song-writer; *USA Today* bestselling author; and his wife, Laney, mother of 7 (6 on earth, 1 in heaven)

The gift of mercy is a rare jewel in a world that keeps such stringent score. This book is a gentle invitation to come and receive that gift and be embraced as you are. It's grace and mercy that changes us, and the words of our friend Craig will pour grace over your soul as you journey through these pages.

MATT AND SARAH HAMMITT, Grammy-nominated singer/song-writer; 3x Dove Award recipient; author/speaker; and his wife, Sarah, mother of 4

When I invited Craig to speak at a weekend service in our church, I had no idea how much I would be encouraged. Too often, my story is defined by measuring up and my worth determined by my productivity. It's exhausting and impossible to maintain. But Craig shared a different story. It was a story of good news that God loves us right where we are, that we are valued and desired, and that God is for us. Learning to live in this truth is absolute freedom. This is Craig's heart message. In *Overflowing Mercies*, we are invited to walk with Craig, to slow down for a few minutes each day and saturate ourselves in the Scriptures and in prayer that we may experience the freedom and rest God offers as we are continually conformed to the image of Jesus.

DON DODGE, Lead Pastor of Avalon Church, Orlando, FL

I have known Craig as a speaker, writer, and friend, and he consistently demonstrates authentic joy rooted in his daily walk with the Lord. *Overflowing Mercies* offers a meaningful experience of God's heart with simple but beautiful language that is approachable for all. Each meditation invites intimacy with the Lord that is profound and personal, whether in an individual, family, or small group setting. As part of an organization that equips men to know God deeper, I am excited to recommend this as a practical resource to guide them on their journey!

JUSTIN WATKINS, Chief Generosity Mentor at Men of Iron

I can vividly remember hearing Craig share his testimony at church after he had committed his life to Jesus as a college freshman in 1995. Since then, we have served as pastors together in three different churches—I can faithfully attest that *Overflowing Mercies* is the overflow of the deep devotional life of a man who walks closely with the Lord throughout all the highs and lows of life. There are treasures in this book for all who read it. Here is both an example and a means of grace to help you grow in your relationship with the Lord!

HOWARD VARNEDOE, Lead Pastor of Hope Community Church, Columbia/Spring Hill, TN

We discovered Craig and Walker's book *Glad You're Here* and resonated so deeply with its message that, when we got married, we gave the book to everyone who came to our wedding. And then we invited Craig to share this message with our church. We aspire to the same way of living that Craig does—he is such a gifted encourager of people. So, when he wrote this devotional book, we knew it would be written by someone coming from a deep place of love for both God and people. And that is exactly what it is. Make it a daily habit for 100 days and you will see God use it to change both your heart and your life!

JEREL AND LIZ LAW, Lead Pastor of Love Lake Norman and fiction author; and his wife, Liz, author and advocate for the marginalized

OVERFLOWING MERCIES

100 MEDITATIONS ON THE TENDER HEART OF GOD

CRAIG ALLEN COOPER

MOODY PUBLISHERS
CHICAGO

Unless otherwise marked, Scripture quotations are from the ESV® Bible (The Holy Bible, English Standard Version®), copyright © 2001 by Crossway, a publishing ministry of Good News Publishers. Used by permission. All rights reserved. The ESV text may not be quoted in any publication made available to the public by a Creative Commons license. The ESV may not be translated in whole or in part into any other language.

Scripture quotations marked (NIV) are taken from the Holy Bible, New International Version®, NIV®. Copyright © 1973, 1978, 1984, 2011 by Biblica, Inc.™ Used by permission of Zondervan. All rights reserved worldwide. www.zondervan.com The "NIV" and "New International Version" are trademarks registered in the United States Patent and Trademark Office by Biblica, Inc.™

All emphasis in Scripture has been added.

Edited by Pamela J. Pugh
Interior design: Brandi Davis
Cover design: Erik M. Peterson
Cover photo of waterfall copyright © 2023 by Christian Tisdale/Stocksy (1807349). All rights reserved.

Library of Congress Cataloging-in-Publication Data

Names: Cooper, Craig Allen, author.
Title: Overflowing mercies : 100 meditations on the tender heart of God / Craig Allen Cooper.
Description: Chicago : Moody Publishers, [2024] | Includes bibliographical references. | Summary: "In this 100-day devotional, you'll be comforted as you meditate on God's character. You'll find courage in His promises to you. And as you soak deeply in God's love and compassion, you'll become better equipped to love and bless the family, friends, and people God has placed in your life"-- Provided by publisher.
Identifiers: LCCN 2023035520 (print) | LCCN 2023035521 (ebook) | ISBN 9780802432698 | ISBN 9780802472793 (ebook)
Subjects: LCSH: God (Christianity)--Mercy. | God--Promises--Biblical teaching. | Devotional exercises. | Meditation. | Prayers. | BISAC: RELIGION / Christian Living / Devotional | RELIGION / Christian Living / Inspirational
Classification: LCC BT153.M4 C66 2024 (print) | LCC BT153.M4 (ebook) | DDC 231/.6--dc23/eng/20231023
LC record available at https://lccn.loc.gov/2023035520
LC ebook record available at https://lccn.loc.gov/2023035521

Originally delivered by fleets of horse-drawn wagons, the affordable paperbacks from D. L. Moody's publishing house resourced the church and served everyday people. Now, after more than 125 years of publishing and ministry, Moody Publishers' mission remains the same—even if our delivery systems have changed a bit. For more information on other books (and resources) created from a biblical perspective, go to www.moodypublishers.com or write to:

Moody Publishers
820 N. LaSalle Boulevard
Chicago, IL 60610

1 3 5 7 9 10 8 6 4 2

Printed in the United States of America

For Laura, Karis, Joshua, Charlotte, and Penelope.
Thank you for filling our home with tender mercy.

Contents

A Note to the Reader 10

1. Mercy Over All 12
2. To All Who Are Thirsty 14
3. Goodness Waiting for You 16
4. Everlasting Arms 18
5. Unmatched Affection 20
6. Your Need and His Provision 22
7. So Much to Look Forward To 24
8. Where Joy Is Found 26
9. God's Usual Way 28
10. Feel the Relief 30
11. God's Heart for You 32
12. The Presence of a Storm 34
13. All the Accomplishment You Will Ever Need 36
14. When All Else Is Stripped Away 38
15. Unwavering Love 40
16. Satisfaction from Above 42
17. Inexhaustible Grace 44
18. How to Fight Your Fear 46
19. God Changes Seasons 48
20. Tell It to the Lord 50
21. When You Feel Weak 52
22. When You Feel Anxious 54
23. Jesus Understands Your Pain 56
24. Your Labor Is Not in Vain 58
25. Our Work and God's Work 60
26. Greatly Loved 62

27. Replenished 64

28. Reassurance for Restless Souls 66

29. Under the Smile of God 68

30. Out of Gas 70

31. Riches for All 72

32. Attracting Favor 74

33. The Attention of God 76

34. Pour It Out 78

35. Driven into His Arms 80

36. Straining Forward 82

37. Comfort in Affliction 84

38. When You Don't Feel Up for It 86

39. The Greatest Display of Strength 88

40. When God Is on Your Side 90

41. Unending Mercies 92

42. Distress, Dread, and Our Deliverer 94

43. The Reason Jesus Came 96

44. A Very Present Help in Trouble 98

45. Who Salvation Belongs To 100

46. Nevertheless 102

47. Sustained in Every Season 104

48. The Rearview Mirror 106

49. The Tender Mercy of God's Watchful Eye 108

50. The Path to Perfect Peace 110

51. Divine Delays 112

52. Faultless 114

53. The Grace I Need 116

54. Every Gift from God 118

55. What Jesus Is Preparing for Us 120

56. What Jesus Wants 122

57. A Mark of Spiritual Vitality 124

58. God Never Wastes Your Pain 126

59. You Cannot Out-Give God 128

60. Crying Out with Cracked Lips 130

61. The Paradox of the Believer's Life 132

62. Invited to Receive 134

63. Wisdom from Above 136

64. Remembering Jesus 138

65. Comfort in a Culture of Criticism 140

66. God Is Not Like Us 142

67. From God's Perspective 144

68. Still, There Is Room 146

69. The Tender Mercy of Our God 148

70. What God Gives 150

71. Peace with God, Purpose in Life 152

72. Suffering for Righteousness' Sake 154

73. The Greatest Act of Kindness We Can Give 156

74. Blessed in Christ 158

75. When You're Dazed and Confused 160

76. What *God* Is Waiting For 162

77. For the Soul That Needs Reviving 164

78. Over the Raging of the Sea 166

79. When We Can't Trace God's Hand 168

80. Looking Up 170

81. When You Don't Know What to Do 172

82. The Origin of All Ministry 174

83. Don't Be Surprised 176

84. The Warmth of the Sun 178

85. How God *Never* Feels 180

86. The God of Hope 182

87. What We Were Made For 184

88. The Secret to Contentment 186

89. Again, Again, and Again 188

90. The Reason We Persevere 190

91. Blessed to Bless 192

92. Tenderhearted 194

93. More than Enough 196

94. The Lord Is Near 198

95. Mercy Unrestrained 200

96. Return 202

97. The God of Unshakable Peace 204

98. The Door of Mercy 206

99. All Things New 208

100. Multiplied 210

Acknowledgments 212

A Note to the Reader

God's love for you is mesmerizing. It is more astonishing than all the wonders of the world and grandeur of the galaxies combined. Anything beautiful or magnificent in creation that has ever stolen your breath away is but a whisper of God's glory that is meant to disclose His ardent and tender affection *for you*.

You are relentlessly on the mind of God, and you are incessantly in the heart of God. If you could fathom in some small way how warmly God truly *feels* about you, the faintest grasp of His immeasurable affection would reduce you to tearful wonder and heartfelt gratitude. It would also make an extraordinary impact on the way you live your life and the way you love those within your relational spheres.

This is the aim of *Overflowing Mercies*: to unveil the tender heart of God *for you*. This work is written as a devotional book, intended to aid the reader in communion with God. For some, this will be an introduction to scriptural meditation. (If communion with God is new to you, my prayer is that as you read the entries in this book, they would be like kindling for your soul, sparking a love for God and His Word that will draw you into the Bible itself in a transformative way that you have never experienced before.)

For others who may be accustomed to reading devotional books, my goal has been to provide you with an additional resource that will serve as a means of comfort, strength, and encouragement to you, with its 100 daily entries on God's tender mercy. Who doesn't need more comfort? Who couldn't use more strength? Do you know anyone too encouraged? I sure don't.

Here are three suggested uses for *Overflowing Mercies*:

Personal Devotions—This book is intended to be read alongside the Bible. My hope is that every entry whets your appetite for more of Scripture. Each entry includes scriptural references, and I invite you to look them up, study them in depth, and see for yourself the treasures in God's Word.

Family/Dinner Table Devotions—For years, our family has benefited from devotional helps for dinner table discussions. After a meal, we may read an entry of a devotional book and ask a question or two to spark spiritual conversations. I am grateful for the resources that have served our family in this way, and I pray that *Overflowing Mercies* will be of similar help to other families. I've included at least one question for reflection after each entry to help guide these types of discussions.

Small Group Encouragement—Any of these meditations can be read at the beginning of a small group meeting to quickly direct the group's attention to God's heart for us in Jesus.

However you choose to use this book, my prayer is "that you, being rooted and grounded in love, may have strength to comprehend with all the saints what is the breadth and length and height and depth, and to know the love of Christ that surpasses knowledge, that you may be filled with all the fullness of God" (Eph. 3:17–19).

1   *Mercy Over All*

PSALM 145:8–9

---

*The LORD is gracious and merciful, slow to anger and abounding in
steadfast love.
The LORD is good to all, and his mercy is over all that he has made.*

G od's inmost heart for you is one of grace, mercy, goodness, and
love. The Lord is not ashamed of you. He is not embarrassed by
you. God is not quick-tempered toward your faults. He is not put off
by your quirks and idiosyncrasies. Yes, in His omniscience, God is fully
aware of everything about you, and nothing is hidden from Him (Heb.
4:13). Yet each one of your weaknesses, faults, frailties, and failures does
more to arouse God's love than to stir up His anger.

Every single day, the Lord showers you with goodness from above
and mercy from His heart of unshakable love. Consider His mercies:
the very breath you are breathing testifies to the goodness of the Lord
in your life; every gasp of air proclaims His great love for you. "He himself gives to all mankind life and breath and everything [else]" (Acts
17:25). Even when you have been unfaithful to Him, hasn't He been
good to you? Even when you've been thankless, hasn't He greeted you
in the morning with favor that you could never earn? Hasn't He protected
you throughout the day from the fullness of what your actions have truly
deserved?

Every blessing in your life is meant to draw your attention to God's
gracious and merciful heart of goodness and love directed toward you.
Yes, you. "The LORD is good to *all*, and his mercy is over *all* that he has
made." *All* includes *you*. Friend, the Lord loves you. Don't think that His
love for you is an afterthought. No, "God shows his love for us in that
while we were still sinners, Christ died for us" (Rom. 5:8). God's love is

an honest love, amid the full knowledge of the worst about us. It's a purposeful, passionate, persistent, and perpetual love.

Oh, that you would trace His gracious heart for you and embrace His immeasurable love for you. God is "abounding in steadfast love" for *you*. Embrace His love with the eyes of faith and love Him in response.

Reflect

Where do you see marks of God's grace, mercy, goodness, and love in your life right now? How do you respond? Check out 1 John 4:19.

Let's Pray

Gracious God, thank You for loving me so much. Thank You for the breath You've given me, the life You've given me, and the mercy You've showered on me. Even in the midst of all my unfaithfulness, You've been faithful to me, and I'm so grateful for Your grace, mercy, patience, and love. Thank You, Lord. In Jesus' name, amen.

2   *To All Who Are Thirsty*

ISAIAH 55:1

Come, everyone who thirsts,
come to the waters;
and he who has no money,
come, buy and eat!
Come, buy wine and milk
without money and without price.

Those who view God as a disinterested, standoffish, harsh ruler with a "you-better-get-your-act-together" kind of attitude and posture will do everything they can to stay away from Him. They will not approach God to relate with Him, and they will not draw near with their spiritual needs and desires. They will be like the man who received the one piece of money he was entrusted with and came forward to account for it upon the Master's return, saying, "I knew you to be a hard man, reaping where you did not sow, and gathering where you scattered no seed, so I was afraid, and I went and hid your talent in the ground" (Matt. 25:24–25). Hard views of God are a breeding ground for fear and hiding. They also lead to ultimate separation from God (Matt. 25:30).

But this is not God's heart for you at all. The true heart of God is one of compassion and tenderness, of open-arms invitation, and of promised blessings to any and all who come to Him. The invitation is *urgent*. See the call to "come" four times here in this one verse from Isaiah above. Our God bids you to come! He welcomes you with arms of mercy, and all you must do to receive that mercy is come to Him, just as you are. This invitation is *universal*. It is for "everyone who thirsts." Everyone means *every one*, and that includes you, dear reader. When all you have to bring to God is your own spiritual thirst and need, He welcomes you and receives you with compassionate open arms.

The invitation is also *generous*: "He who has no money, come, buy and eat!" You don't have to bring any offering other than your need. Here's all the invitation your thirsty soul needs: "Come ... come ... come ... come." All you have to do is come to Him. If you feel that your soul is hungry and you sense that your spirit is thirsty, you are most blessed of God, as it is *you* who are invited to "come." Jesus said, "Blessed are those who hunger and thirst for righteousness, for they shall be satisfied" (Matt. 5:6). He also said, "I am the bread of life; whoever comes to me shall not hunger, and whoever believes in me shall never thirst" (John 6:35).

Reflect

How does this invitation *from* God change your view *of* God? How will you respond as a result?

Let's Pray

Lord, I come to You with the empty arms of faith, bringing nothing but my need, my arms stretched out for Your mercy. Thank You for inviting the thirsty to come and drink, the hungry to come and feast. Thank You for inviting the spiritually poor to come and receive. Just as I am, I come to You. Please satisfy me in Your presence. In Jesus' name, amen.

3   *Goodness Waiting for You*

PSALM 31:19

Oh, how abundant is your goodness, which you have stored up for those who fear you.

Dear believer, because of the truth of this verse, you can banish every foreboding thought and every imagination of impending doom. Our gracious God has emphatically expressed His heart for you in our text this day. Here's what God has ready and waiting for your future: *His goodness.*

When Moses prayed, "Please show me your glory," the Lord responded saying, "I will make all my goodness pass before you" (Ex. 33:18–19). What is amazing is that we see the glory of God most clearly in His goodness directed toward us. We have that goodness expressed in our text in future tense; it is a goodness that has been "stored up" for those who fear the Lord. Believer, God's goodness is waiting for you, as if your name were written on the tag. Think of it! You have an inheritance of *goodness* being held specifically for you. Every morsel is yours to receive, yours to enjoy, yours to honor your Lord with, so identified to your individual personhood that it is as much your possession now as if you held it in your hands in this present moment.

And notice this description: "How *abundant* is your goodness." What a wealth of grace is in this one word, *abundant*! The goodness God has in store for you is more than enough! It's a cornucopia of plentiful, nourishing, overflowing favor that has been expressly set aside for you. Yours is the promise of future goodness and everlasting mercy and grace. The psalmist exclaims, "Surely goodness and mercy shall follow me all the days of my life, and I shall dwell in the house of the LORD forever" (Ps. 23:6).

May this promise of forthcoming goodness, which is more than enough for you now and for all eternity, be a ray of light to warm the frigidity from your soul and incline your sighing spirit to sing amidst the cloudiest of days: "Oh, how abundant is your goodness, which you have stored up for those who fear you."

Reflect

When you think about the future, do you typically imagine the goodness of God or something else? How does the truth of this psalm change your perspective of what's in store for you in the days to come?

Let's Pray

Lord, thank You that You have goodness in store for me, set aside for me, and waiting for me and for all who fear and trust in You. Please show me Your glory! Help me see Your goodness with the eyes of faith and to trust that my future is secure in You. In Jesus' name, amen.

4   *Everlasting Arms*

PSALM 145:14

*The Lord upholds all who are falling
and raises up all who are bowed down.*

Perhaps I am speaking to one who is depressed in soul this very moment. You may feel as if no one on earth can understand what you are wrestling through. After all, "the heart knows its own bitterness, and no stranger shares its joy" (Prov. 14:10). Indeed, at times you would admit that you yourself stand aloof from any comprehension of the cause of the gloominess within your own soul.

Have you wondered, *Why do I wake up sad, heavy-hearted, head full of nothing but doubts and fears? Where is all the joy of my former days?* The psalmist had the same musings: "Has God forgotten to be gracious? Has he in anger shut up his compassion?" (Ps. 77:9). Yes, some of us have known darkness too deep for trivial descriptions. Darkness that breeds only questions, devoid of any answers. What hope is there for you who are not only *not* standing firm, but feel as if you are falling?

Here is comfort for you in your affliction: "The Lord upholds all who are falling and raises up all who are bowed down."

You cannot uphold yourself, *but the Lord upholds you.* "The eternal God is your dwelling place, and underneath are the everlasting arms" (Deut. 33:27a). If you must fall, you will fall into His arms. He who has loved you from eternity past will not let you go, so fall right into His great love for you.

When you have nothing to trust in but the everlasting arms of the eternal God to catch you as you are falling, you have everything you need for this life and for all eternity. The Lord Himself will uphold you who are falling and will raise up every single one who is bowed down

(John 6:39–40). Trust not this day in the state of your emotions, but in the strength of His everlasting arms.

Reflect

How have you experienced the Lord upholding you in the past? Do you feel like you are falling right now? What would it look like for you to fall into the arms of God?

Let's Pray

Lord, I admit that my emotions can be all over the map. One moment, I can be sighing deeply and another moment singing joyfully. I thank You, Lord, that whether I am singing or sighing, "Jesus Christ is the same yesterday and today and forever" (Heb. 13:8). When I am falling, it is You who holds me up. Please hold me up this day and help me find rest and peace in Your everlasting, unfailing arms, for Your glory. In Jesus' name, amen.

5   *Unmatched Affection*

I have been crucified with Christ. It is no longer I who live, but Christ who lives in me. And the life I now live in the flesh I live by faith in the Son of God, who loved me and gave himself for me. I do not nullify the grace of God, for if righteousness were through the law, then Christ died for no purpose.

God's love for you and me does not fluctuate based on our own achievements or accolades. It rests on us in Christ. Christ died for our sins, "the righteous for the unrighteous," to bring us to God (1 Peter 3:18). So believers can now say that they have been crucified with Christ. The Son of God suffered in *our* place. He was condemned that we might be forgiven.

Because of this, we can confidently say that we are loved by God. Go ahead and say this out loud: He "loved *me* and gave himself for *me*" (Gal. 2:20). Hear the significance of these immeasurably powerful words of Christ's personal affection for you. Jesus said, "Greater love has no one than this, that someone lay down his life for his friends" (John 15:13). What more does Jesus need to do to show you that He loves you? He has already done it all! There is no greater love He can express toward you than what He has already done in laying down His life for you, and He calls you friend (John 15:15). Yes, the Lord knows you are a sinner. The good news is that Jesus is a "friend of sinners" (see Matt. 11:19). He laid down His life for His friends who had fallen short of the glory of God (Rom. 3:23–25). This is amazing love, unmatched affection!

Christ sacrificed His perfect life to secure our eternal life. Jesus' love is everlasting, eternal, unceasing, unchanging, steadfast, and unrelenting (Jer. 31:3), and it has *nothing* to do with your own performance, your own good works, or your own achievements. It has everything to do with His own great love, wholly and completely unmerited, unearned, and unalterable, laid down for you.

Take heart, dear friend—Jesus loves you. Rest in His great love. And if you don't yet know this love, do not rest until you can assuredly say, "I have been crucified with Christ. It is no longer I who live, but Christ who lives in me." When Christ is your life, all of time is in your favor, even to eternity. Why would we not surrender in wonder to so great a love?

Reflect

Why was it necessary for Jesus to die to secure our righteousness before God, and how does Jesus' death on the cross display His love for us?

Let's Pray

Jesus, Son of God, I surrender to Your great love. Thank You, Lord, for laying down Your life for me. In view of Your mercy, I freely offer my life back to You. I live by faith now in the Son of God who loved me and gave Himself for me. I love You, Lord, and I am fully Yours, for Your glory. Amen.

6 *Your Need and His Provision*

He regards the prayer of the destitute
and does not despise their prayer.

O my soul, do you feel destitute right now? Do you sense you are in an impoverished state? Do you recognize your need for something greater, for Someone greater? If so, take heart: the Lord regards your prayer. Others may have no regard for you. You may be held as the scum of the earth, the refuse of the world (1 Cor. 4:13). You may even hold little regard for yourself, but take heart: *the Lord regards your prayer.* Our God respects, esteems, and favors the appeals of the destitute. He looks upon the lowly with tender mercy. God's sympathetic gaze is upon the broken, and He honors their prayer (Isa. 66:1–2).

Our text goes further: *He does not despise your prayers.* Others may despise you, but only one opinion matters. God's grace gravitates toward the lowly, toward the lonely, and toward the loathed. Those who feel scorned in the world find favor with the Lord. He does this to show His immeasurable love and so that no one boasts in themselves, but instead all boasting is in the Lord Himself. Jesus alone is our wisdom, our righteousness, and our redemption; all exultation is reserved for Him alone (see 1 Cor. 1:28–31).

Your need qualifies you for *His* provision. "Blessed are the poor in spirit, for theirs is the kingdom of heaven" (Matt. 5:3). Bless God for the sense of scarcity that drives you into His arms for safety! "He who dwells in the shelter of the Most High will abide in the shadow of the Almighty. I will say to the LORD, 'My refuge and my fortress, my God, in whom I trust'" (Ps. 91:1–2).

Far from despising your prayer, the Lord welcomes your cries as He eagerly desires to show you mercy: "Therefore the LORD waits to be gracious to you, and therefore he exalts himself to show mercy to you. For the LORD is a God of justice; blessed are all those who wait for him" (Isa. 30:18).

Your pleas will prompt His provision and awaken His compassion. "Let us then with confidence draw near to the throne of grace, that we may receive mercy and find grace to help in time of need" (Heb. 4:16).

Reflect

Are you ever hesitant to communicate your needs and desires to God in prayer? Does this psalm change your perspective of how God views your prayers?

Let's Pray

Lord, You know my desperate state. I bring my unending need to Your never-failing provision. Thank You for using the hard things of life to drive me to the tenderness of Your mercy. I take refuge in You alone. In Jesus' name, amen.

7　So Much to Look Forward To

But the path of the righteous is like the light of dawn,
which shines brighter and brighter until full day.

Listen carefully to these words of wisdom from Proverbs because there is so much hope for you within these truths! Dear believer, your best life is not *behind you*; your best life is not *right now*; your best is *yet to come*. The path of the righteous is like the light of dawn. As first light shakes off the darkness, it carries with it the promises of an even brighter hour. Dawn is the beginning of a new day, the first appearance of light touching the sky before the sun fully rises, warming the earth.

Your path, your way, your life on this side of eternity is like that light of dawn. Fear not when you consider your future—you have so much to look forward to! Scripture says, "He who began a good work in you will bring it to completion at the day of Jesus Christ" (Phil. 1:6) and "Those who are wise shall shine like the brightness of the sky above" (Dan. 12:3).

So do not look upon *your past* as though your best moments are in the rearview mirror. The author of Ecclesiastes wrote, "Say not, 'Why were the former days better than these?' For it is not from wisdom that you ask this" (Eccl. 7:10). Instead, thank God for the grace you have experienced in the days of old, but thank Him most of all that those past mercies are only a glimmer of the good He has in store for you. Say with the psalmist, "Surely goodness and mercy shall follow me *all the days of my life, and I shall dwell in the house of the* LORD *forever*" (Ps. 23:6).

In the same way, do not look at *your present* as the pinnacle of your days of glory. Now we see as in a mirror dimly, but then we shall see face to face. Now we know in part; then we shall know fully, even as we have been fully known (see 1 Cor. 13:12). Rejoice in this, that *your future* is incredibly bright. Let the knowledge of God's pending glory fill you with gratefulness for every past mercy and every present grace. Today is but the light of dawn! A bright future is coming for all those in Christ, "and night will be no more. They will need no light of lamp or sun, for the Lord God will be their light, and they will reign forever and ever" (Rev. 22:5). It is settled, believer; your best is yet to come!

Reflect

What emotions typically surface in your heart when you think of your past, present, and future?

Let's Pray

Lord, it is so tempting to view the past with rose-colored glasses, as if all my glory days have passed by. It's also so easy to see the challenges of the present and to consider the future with fear. Please give me Your perspective. Help me grasp the hope of future grace and to view the days to come with faith-filled eyes. I believe; help my unbelief. In Jesus' name, amen.

8 *Where Joy Is Found*

PHILIPPIANS 4:4

Rejoice in the Lord always; again I will say, rejoice.

Occasions of joy are sure to come, though they oscillate like the changing of seasons. For our joy to be a constant, it must be grounded in something firmer than our own fluctuating fortunes. If I find no joy in my present circumstances, I can still rejoice in God's presence. As God's presence is with us always, we always have reasons to rejoice (see Matt. 28:20; Heb. 13:5). So what does it look like to rejoice in the Lord?

When we rejoice in the Lord, we rejoice in His *sovereignty*. The Most High rules with absolute authority over the kingdoms of the earth, governing all of history and every detail of our lives (see 1 Chron. 29:12; Ps. 139:13–16). Even when "The lot is cast into the lap, . . . its every decision is from the LORD" (Prov. 16:33). No matter the situation, we can rejoice that the Lord our God is in complete control.

We also rejoice in His *wisdom*. God is boundless in wisdom. We may not understand what He is doing in our lives or in the world, but we can rest in the assurance that He is wisely steering all things toward His glory and the good of His people (see Rom. 8:28). When we rejoice in the wisdom of God, we proclaim with the apostle Paul, "Oh, the depth of the riches and wisdom and knowledge of God! How unsearchable are his judgments and how inscrutable his ways!" (Rom. 11:33).

We can also rejoice in God's perfect *love* at all times. We may not understand what we're going through, but we can trust that God loves us at the bottom of it all. So "in all these things we are more than conquerors through him who loved us. For I am sure that neither death nor life, nor angels nor rulers, nor things present nor things to come, nor powers, nor height nor depth, nor anything else in all creation, will be able to separate us from the love of God in Christ Jesus our Lord" (Rom. 8:37–39).

When we consider the sovereignty, wisdom, and love of God, we can "rejoice in the Lord *always*" because in the Father of lights "there is no variation or shadow due to change" (James 1:17). Our unchanging God is invariably a stable source of steadfast joy.

Believer, take heart this day, and *rejoice in the Lord*!

Reflect

Who do you know whose joy seems untouched by their circumstances? How does their example inspire you?

Let's Pray

Lord, I admit that it is easier for me to rejoice when my circumstances are favorable than when they are challenging, but I want the kind of joy that is untouched by changing circumstances. I want to rejoice in You always. Even when I'm praying for my circumstances to change, I rejoice that You are in complete control, that You are infinite in wisdom, and that You are perfect in Your love. I trust You; I look to You in prayer; and I rejoice in You. Please fill me with Your Spirit and Your joy. In Jesus' name, amen.

9 *God's Usual Way*

Turn to me and be gracious to me, as is your way with those who love your name.

God has a certain way with those who love His name. It does the soul good to know it, to believe it, and to rest in the assurance of it. That way is spelled out for us in our text: He is *favorably inclined* to bless those who love His name.

It's incredible, and it's true! The God who made the heavens and the earth, who created the cosmos and rules over the galaxies, governments, and granular details of our lives is *favorably disposed* toward those who love Him. What could be more assuring than to know that God is for us? As the apostle Paul has expressed so wonderfully in Romans 8:38–39, I, too, am convinced that nothing—neither personal financial woes, nor a global crisis, nor persistent health concerns, nor challenges relationally, nor internal emotional struggles, nor external opposition and ridicule from others, nor anything else in all of creation will be able to separate us from the love of God in Christ Jesus our Lord. Indeed, "if God is for us, who can be against us?" (Rom. 8:31).

So, my soul, do you truly love the Lord? Is He the treasure of your heart? Do you long to know Him more and to enjoy more of His fellowship? Do you *love* Him? If so, you can be assured that *the Lord loves you.* You would not love Him if He had not first loved you as we read in 1 John 4:19. It was God's love for *you* that inspired your love for *Him.* Yours is a responsive love, yet it is a love that is accompanied by the immeasurable blessing of His grace and mercy: "No eye has seen, nor ear heard, nor the heart of man imagined, what God has prepared for those who love him" (1 Cor. 2:9).

God's way toward those who love Him is to bestow His grace and mercy upon them. The Lord turns toward the one who yearns for Him. He doesn't turn *away* from you; He turns *toward* you! The Lord turns toward us with gracious kindness. Even the trials that come our way are designed to be a blessing as Deuteronomy 8:16–17 reminds us. So we can confidently pray with the psalmist, "Turn to me and be gracious to me, as is your way with those who love your name."

Reflect

Do you truly love the Lord? If so, *why* do you love Him, and *what* do you love about Him? Tell Him.

Let's Pray

Lord, I love You. I truly do. I know that I love You because You first loved me. Thank You for loving me even when I was unlovable. I pray, Lord, please turn to me and be gracious to me, since that is Your way with those who love Your name. Help me and comfort me again, Lord; I am Yours. Amen.

10   *Feel the Relief*

Blessed are those whose lawless deeds are forgiven, and whose sins are covered; blessed is the man against whom the Lord will not count his sin.

Anyone whose financial debts had been fully forgiven would not only breathe a sigh of relief but would sing with shouts of joy! Think of it. No more student loan payments, no more car payments, no more house payments, no more credit card statements inducing stress, no more installments, no interest required, no more burden of debt. What a happy day! The one whose debts are forgiven is truly blessed, and the more the indebtedness, the more the joy would be when that debt is fully forgiven.

Dear reader, your greatest burden is not the load of your financial debt, but the weight of your sin against almighty God. "For the wages of sin is death, but the free gift of God is eternal life in Christ Jesus our Lord" (Rom. 6:23). Jesus, the Son of God, came from heaven to earth to pay the debt we owe for our sin, so that we could be fully and freely forgiven. Fully God and fully man, Jesus was born to die in order to save His people from their sins (Matt. 1:21).

Jesus lived the perfect life we could never live, and on the cross of Calvary, He took our place; He received the punishment we deserve for our sins. He bore the wrath of God for all who trust in Him. He paid for our sins in full and purchased forgiveness and eternal life for all who trust in Him. If you have trusted in Christ, you are blessed indeed as Romans 4:7-8 assures us.

If you have not trusted in Christ, all the debt of your sin remains on your shoulders, and you will have to pay. Yet God invites you into this blessing of forgiveness right now. Why not call on Him now and let the weight of your sins fall off your shoulders as you perceive them landing squarely on the shoulders of Christ Jesus? *You,* too, can enter into this free, full, and forever forgiveness: Everyone is welcome. Everyone is invited. "Everyone who calls on the name of the Lord will be saved" (see Rom. 10:12–13).

Reflect

Have you ever had a massive debt paid? If so, what emotions did you experience when that happened? If not, what emotions could you imagine experiencing to be completely debt-free? Have you had your sins forgiven through faith in Christ? If not, why not ask Him for that gift right now?

Let's Pray

Merciful God, thank You for sending Your Son as my Savior, to take the punishment that I deserved, to pay the debt that I owed. That my debts can be fully and forever forgiven is incredible mercy! I'm so grateful, Lord. Please help me realize the glory of this good news and walk in the good of it. My life is Yours. In Jesus' name, amen.

11 *God's Heart for You*

He (Jesus) said also to the man who had invited him, "When you give a dinner or a banquet, do not invite your friends or your brothers or your relatives or rich neighbors, lest they also invite you in return and you be repaid. But when you give a feast, invite the poor, the crippled, the lame, the blind, and you will be blessed, because they cannot repay you. For you will be repaid at the resurrection of the just."

L ife is hard, and we err when we take the hard stuff of life and equate it to the heart of God as if God takes delight in our troubles. We may often struggle to believe that God's heart toward us is graciously inclined, favorably disposed, eagerly leaning forward to bless with a spare-no-expense disposition of mercy and kindness. But what we see here is that God has invited those who could never repay to feast at His table of His mercy and grace.

Several years ago, my wife, Laura, and I celebrated our fortieth birthdays with an epic trip up scenic Route 1 along the coast of California. Traveling from southern California to northern California, curving around the rocky shore of Big Sur, was incredibly breathtaking. After that trip, we were determined to travel back to California, and a few years later, we did.

Arriving in northern California, we were thrilled by the invitation to join a dinner party at a restaurant that had previously been ranked the top in the world. There we were, treated to what may be the finest meal we have ever enjoyed this side of heaven. Now, this restaurant was not something we could readily afford, but we gratefully accepted the invitation, joined the group, and were absolutely blown away by the extravagance of every detail of that evening and the meal we enjoyed at the full expense of our gracious host.

We left with a gift, a clothespin with the name of the restaurant type-set on it, given as a souvenir to help the guests remember that evening's experience. Laura handed it to me, and she said, "Craig, remember, this is God's heart for *you*: extravagant affection." The Lord loves us with lavish love, bountiful goodness, and tender mercy. Believe it. Receive it. Enjoy it. That's God's heart for you.

Reflect

Do you struggle to believe that God's heart toward you is graciously inclined, favorably disposed, and eagerly leaning forward to bless you with a spare-no-expense type of kindness? How does this meditation encourage your faith in God's grace toward you?

Let's Pray

Lord, thank You for inviting the poor, the crippled, the lame, the blind, and the needy to come feast at the table of Your grace and mercy. You didn't invite those who could repay You to join You at Your table; You invited the needy to shower them with mercy. Thank You for saving a seat for me at Your table. I accept Your invitation and relish Your tender mercy. In Jesus' name, amen.

12 *The Presence of a Storm*

MARK 6:50-51

Immediately he spoke to them and said, "Take heart; it is I. Do not be afraid." And he got into the boat with them, and the wind ceased. And they were utterly astounded.

Here, Jesus made His disciples get into a boat and go before Him to the other side, while He dismissed the crowd and went up to the mountain to pray (Mark 6:45–46). We know from the rest of the passage that a storm is coming. So here Jesus is, in essence, sending His disciples into a storm. And yet, we see that this is a loving act in light of how He reveals His glory to them.

Sometimes Jesus leads us *into* a storm. He sends us into the raging tempest for reasons we can't fully understand, but it is then that He draws near to reveal Himself to us in power. Jesus is sovereign over every storm. First He *sent* His disciples into the storm (v. 45), then He *saw* His disciples making headway painfully, with the wind against them (v. 48a); He *watched over* them during the fourth watch of the night (v. 48b); and wonderfully, He came to them, and when Jesus came, He came walking on the sea (v. 48c).

Jesus' watching does not mean that no trouble will come our way, but it does mean no trouble will come to us that is outside of His control and perfect design (Ps. 91:9–14). The presence of a storm does not mean the absence of God. Jesus said, "In this world you will have trouble. But take heart! I have overcome the world" (John 16:33 NIV).

The "fourth watch" of the night is between 3 a.m. and 6 a.m., a time when, undoubtedly, the disciples would have been utterly exhausted and completely depleted. Sometimes God delays His deliverance to drive us in dependence back to Himself and to display His glory in profound ways. When we've got nothing left, *He comes*. He is often *the God of the fourth watch of the night*.

Jesus' coming *is* always calming. The turmoil within our souls is put to rest in the presence of the Almighty. "Take heart; it is I" is the Greek phrase equivalent to the same expression God used to reveal Himself to Moses: "I AM WHO I AM." Jesus is saying here, "Take heart. *I AM*. Do not be afraid." If the Lord who rules over the raging of the sea is with us and on our side, what do we have to fear? Jesus draws near to the storm-tossed and the washed-out, and He calms the storm. May He calm the storm raging in your soul this day, for His glory.

Reflect

Can you think of a time when you've experienced the presence of God during a storm in your own life? How did the Lord draw near to you in the storm?

Let's Pray

Lord, thank You that You rule over the raging seas, that You are on my side, that You hear my prayers, that You come to me in the fourth watch of the night when I'm utterly exhausted and completely depleted, and You come walking on the water, calming the storm and stilling the furious sea. Help me to not give in to fear, and please show me Your power. All my trust is in You, Lord. In Jesus' name I pray. Amen.

13 *All the Accomplishment You Will Ever Need*

JOHN 19:30

"It is finished."

These three words strung together on the lips of the crucified Savior carry more wealth than if every ocean were full of gold. Jesus victoriously announces the successful completion of the work He was sent by God the Father to do on our behalf.

Jesus came to live the life we could never live, perfectly fulfilling the law of God on our behalf (Matt. 5:17), and to die as a substitute in our place, securing for us forgiveness and the gift of eternal life (John 3:14–17). Now, we who have trusted in the Savior can say along with the apostle that "I have been crucified with Christ. It is no longer I who live, but Christ who lives in me. And the life I now live in the flesh I live by faith in the Son of God, who loved me and gave himself for me. I do not nullify the grace of God, for if righteousness were through the law, then Christ died for no purpose" (Gal. 2:20–21).

To purpose to add *anything* to the finished work of Christ as a basis for our acceptance before God is to detract *everything* from the finished work of Christ. We either trust in Christ completely or we do not trust in Him at all. God does not accept us because of our own good works, church attendance, acts of service, baptism, community involvement, faithfully checked-off to-do lists, or because of anything that we have or haven't done. Any acceptance with God is based on Christ's righteousness, not our own. This is good news for flawed people who do not have their act completely together (or together at all!).

Jesus said, "It is finished." All the work that needed to be done for our redemption has been completed *in Him*. Christ is now risen from the grave and has ascended on high and He is seated at the right hand of the throne of God and ever lives to make intercession for His own (Heb. 7:25). He has promised to never leave us and never forsake us. He is eternally *for us* (Heb. 13:5b; Matt. 28:20; Rom. 8:31). This is the rest we achievers truly long to embrace.

Believer, in Christ you have been set free from the bondage of living for the fluctuating approval of others or the fleeting glory of your own accomplishments. In Jesus and Jesus *alone* is all the approval and all the accomplishment you will ever need! Let that sink in to the core of your being.

Think stunningly of *His perfection*. Can you add to it? No. Can you detract from it? No. It is flawless, faultless, *finished* perfection. It is a completed work. Now, you can wholly glory in what Christ has accomplished *for you*. You do not need to perform or achieve *anything* to earn God's acceptance. Jesus is your righteousness, and all the approval you'll ever need is found in Him. Now, may your love for God and others display the gratitude of one amazed to be saved by grace alone!

Reflect

What emotions do you experience when you contemplate the finished work of Jesus on your behalf?

Let's Pray

Lord Jesus, thank You for living the perfect life I could never live, for faultlessly fulfilling the law of God on my behalf, for dying on the cross as a substitute in my place, and for securing my forgiveness and the gift of eternal life. You did all the work that was necessary for my salvation, and You have said, "It is finished." Ah, thank You, Lord! I worship You and gratefully rest in Your finished work on my behalf! Amen.

14   *When All Else Is Stripped Away*

PSALM 16:5–6

The LORD is my chosen portion and my cup;
you hold my lot.
The lines have fallen for me in pleasant places;
indeed, I have a beautiful inheritance.

This psalm of David shows that his joy was not first and foremost in the gifts God had given him, but in God Himself; this is instructive for us because the greatest gift we can receive is a relationship with the Lord.

David called *God* his portion and his cup. This is a creative way of saying that God was the source of all sustenance in his life, his food and his drink. It's as if David was proclaiming, "Lord, if I have You and nothing else, I have everything I ever need. You are my bread, my life, my joy, my peace, and my everything. You're all I desire, and I'll survive on *You*." What an expression of contentment of soul!

This may very well have been written during the time when David was on the run from Saul, unjustly driven away by the fury of a jealous king. Yet David sings that the lines have fallen for him in *pleasant* places. He was wondrously aware that though he may have lost access to his home, he had not lost access to God, and that was enough to sustain him even while he was on the run. No one could take from David his relationship with God; even as a fugitive, he was able to rejoice because his joy was in the Lord.

When everything else is stripped away and all our creature comforts are gone, we're reminded of what truly matters most. The contented soul looks at what is inside the boundary lines of God's grace and remembers that whatever else is lost, our relationship with the Lord falls inside those boundary lines of His grace. We may lose all of our life's savings and all of our securities, but we cannot lose our Savior and His presence; we are forever safe in His hands (John 10:28 29). In Christ, we have peace with God. In Christ, we have the promise of the presence of God. In Christ, we've been forgiven of *all* our sins. In Christ, our names have been written in heaven. In Christ, we have the hope of eternal life. Indeed, the boundary lines have fallen for us in pleasant places, and we have a beautiful inheritance!

Happy is the trouble that drives us trembling back into the arms of the heavenly Father. That's right where we belong. Let's delight ourselves in the Lord who is our portion.

Reflect

Do you tend to focus more on what's inside the boundary lines of God's grace for you, or what's outside? Is there anything you feel like you can't live without in this life? Can you say with David, "The LORD is my chosen portion and my cup"?

Let's Pray

Father, You are all I need. If I have You and nothing else, I have everything. If I have everything the world could offer, and I don't have You, I have nothing. Thank You for the gift of a relationship with You. Thank You, Father, for sending Your Son, Jesus, to rescue and redeem me and hold me fast forevermore. You are my portion, and all my joy in this life and for all eternity is found in You. In Jesus' name I pray. Amen.

15   *Unwavering Love*

*"I have loved you with an everlasting love;
therefore I have continued my faithfulness to you."*

G od's love for you doesn't fluctuate like the weather. It's not warm and sunny one day and then cold and dreary the next. It's not up and down, *for it's an everlasting love.* Because God's love is from everlasting, *it's not based on your performance.* God set His affections on you long before you ever set your affections on Him. "Blessed be the God and Father of our Lord Jesus Christ, who has blessed us in Christ with every spiritual blessing in the heavenly places, even as he chose us in him *before the foundation of the world,* that we should be holy and blameless before him" (Eph. 1:3–4).

The Lord loves you with an everlasting love. Because it's everlasting, it is eternal. You may say, "But you don't know the evil I've done, the sins I've committed." To that the Lord assures you, by showing "his love for us in that *while we were still sinners, Christ died for us*" (Rom. 5:8). It's true that your obedience, your performance, and your faithfulness are up and down like a yo-yo. They oscillate like the weather, hot one day and cold the next . . . but listen carefully, dear believer, *that's not the way God's love is.* God's love for you is a fixed and eternal love. It is from everlasting to everlasting, so it does not waver like yours (and mine) does.

If God's love for you was based on anything good or bad that you have done, it would be an erratic love. But our text says it's *an everlasting love.* You may be up and down, but the Lord never changes. Indeed, "Jesus Christ is the same yesterday and today and forever" (Heb. 13:8). So take a deep breath and let your soul soak in this peace of God's immutable, unchanging, everlasting love. Look up into the sky and see if you can see the end of it. You can't, and neither will you be able to discover the end of God's love: "For as high as the heavens are above the earth, so great is his steadfast love toward those who fear him" (Ps. 103:11).

Take heart: from everlasting to everlasting, you are loved by God above.

Reflect

Do you tend to think God loves you based on your performance? How so? How does this meditation change your view of the love of God for you?

Let's Pray

O Lord, can it truly be that You love me with an everlasting love? What incredible grace and mercy! Thank You for not pointing to my performance as the basis of my acceptance with You. If Your love for me were based on my performance, it would be so unpredictable, so inconsistent, and so often nonexistent, but that's not how You love me. You love me in Jesus—based on His perfect life. Thank You, Lord! Help me live a life that reflects Your steadfast love, which never changes, and Your mercies, which never come to an end. For Your glory. In Jesus' name, amen.

16 *Satisfaction from Above*

PSALM 81:10

Open your mouth wide, and I will fill it.

Baby birds beg their fathers and mothers for food by opening their mouths wide and squealing as loudly as they can. Hatchlings have colorful gapes that draw the attention of their parents, alerting the parents of their babies' hunger. If you're ever around a nest of baby birds, you will notice their mouths open wide at the arrival of an adult to the nest. In the early days of the bird's life, there is not much else they can do. Squeal, squawk, plead, and wait for the parent bird to fill their mouths with food.

The Lord says here, "Open your mouth wide, and I will fill it." This is a generous promise that if we come to God for satisfaction, He will satisfy us. The Lord is our provider. We can come to Him with every necessity and every request and He "will supply every need of yours according to his riches in glory in Christ Jesus" (Phil. 4:19). Remember what Jesus said in Matthew 6:31–33: to not be anxious about what you'll eat or drink or wear because "your heavenly Father knows that you need them all." Instead, "seek first the kingdom of God and his righteousness," and all your other necessities will be provided as well.

Not only does God promise to supply our needs, but He also promises here to satisfy us with pleasure. "But he would feed you with the finest of the wheat, and with honey from the rock I would satisfy you" (Ps. 81:16). The finest wheat, delicious honey . . . provision, pleasure, and satisfaction will be delivered to the one who looks to God as their source of delight and seeks Him as their greatest treasure. What a promise!

You make known to me the path of life;

> in your presence there is fullness of joy;
>
> at your right hand are pleasures forevermore. (Ps. 16:11)

Reflect

Where do you typically run for pleasure, safety, and satisfaction? How can you run to God for all these things?

Let's Pray

Father, You know my needs, my cravings, my desires. You know my tendencies, my habits, all my straying and returning. Please incline my heart to seek its joy and satisfaction in You and to enjoy what You provide in a way that honors You. Lord, I open wide my mouth for more of You. I want to look from the gifts to the Giver and glory in You alone. In Your presence is fullness of joy and at Your right hand are pleasures forevermore. I love you. In Jesus' name, amen.

17 *Inexhaustible Grace*

2 CORINTHIANS 9:8

And God is able to make all grace abound to you, so that having all sufficiency in all things at all times, you may abound in every good work.

This is one of my favorite verses in all the Bible. Here is encouragement and assurance to the highest degree! God's grace is *inexhaustible*—an unlimited wealth of support, boundless kindness, lavish generosity, and overflowing mercies from above. Ponder the superlative nature of these promises in our text: God is able to make *all* grace *abound* to you, that having *all* sufficiency in *all* things at *all* times, you may *abound* in *every* good work. This is abounding grace to its maximum level.

God's grace is a deluge, not a drip.

It's a downpour, not a trickle.

It's a mighty waterfall, not a sprinkle.

This is a fountain of goodness that never runs dry. You and I do not have a need for grace that God cannot supply. What is it that you need today? What form of grace are you lacking? Look to the Possessor of all grace and know that He is the most generous of all beings! Jesus said of the heavenly Father,

> Ask, and it will be given to you; seek, and you will find; knock, and it will be opened to you. For everyone who asks receives, and the one who seeks finds, and to the one who knocks it will be opened. Or which one of you, if his son asks him for bread, will give him a stone? Or if he asks for a fish, will give him a serpent? If you then, who are evil, know how to give good gifts to your children, how much more will your Father who is in heaven give good things to those who ask him! (Matt.7:7–11)

My soul, lay your request before the One who is eager to supply your needs, knowing that it is to the Father's glory that you bear much fruit, showing yourself to be a disciple of Jesus. As Jesus has said, when we remain in Him and His words remain in us, we can ask whatever we wish and it will be done for us. God is glorified in us when we bear spiritual fruit as we depend on Him (see John 15:7–10).

Reflect

How does it encourage, comfort, and strengthen your soul to know that God is able to make all grace abound to you? What kind of grace do you need *right now*? Let your request be made known to God and watch how He supplies.

Let's Pray

Father, I praise You for your inexhaustible riches of grace and mercy. Thank You that there is no need that You cannot meet, no want that You cannot supply. Thank You that You are able to make all grace abound to me, so that in all things, at all times, having all that I need, I will abound in every good work. Lord, You know exactly what I need this moment, this day, this season. Please open up the floodgates of heaven and pour out Your Spirit and Your supplies of grace for everything You have called me to do, for Your glory. I trust in You completely. In Jesus' name, amen.

18 *How to Fight Your Fear*

PSALM 56:3-4

When I am afraid, I put my trust in you.
In God, whose word I praise, in God I trust; I shall not be afraid.
What can flesh do to me?

For all of us who struggle with fear, here is a lifeline of tender mercy. We are not alone in our fears. David conquered the lion and the bear and the giant Goliath. Yet even this titan of faith struggled with his own fears—Psalm 56 was born from a moment of terror when, on the run from King Saul, he was seized by enemies in a place called Gath. David had been fleeing from King Saul because Saul had expressly threatened to kill him (see 1 Sam. 20:31), but David was also known as the mighty warrior who had slain tens of thousands of Philistines, so the Philistines did not take too kindly to having him in their hometown (1 Sam. 21:10–15). Everywhere he turned, David's life was being threatened. Yet in the midst of his fears, he knew and trusted that God would not leave him alone. So mercifully, in this text, we have David's own battle plan for fighting the goliath of fear, and we can adopt the strategy for our own fearful hearts as well.

First, David *recognizes his fear*: "When I am afraid." He didn't ignore his fear. He didn't minimize it. He didn't lie to himself and pretend it wasn't there. He simply and humbly recognized the fear, called it for what it was, and acknowledged its presence. But he didn't stop there.

David *redirects his focus*. Notice the way David turns his full attention *Godward*: "I put my trust in you. In God, whose word I praise, in God I trust." Three times in two verses, David speaks of the Lord. He is praying in this psalm, addressing the Lord: "I put my trust *in you*."

Finally, David *resists his fear with faith*: "I shall not be afraid." Here is trust in God, reliance upon God's Word, and refuge in God's authority. David contrasts God's sovereignty with man's cruelty under the banner of truth that God is in complete control. What's his conclusion after this meditation? Here it is: "What can flesh do to me?"

Fearful saint, this is a proven, three-part strategy for fighting the giant of anxiety: recognize your fear, redirect your focus, resist your fear with faith.

God is on your side. And "what then shall we say to these things? If God is for us, who can be against us?" (Rom. 8:31).

Reflect

How does fear manifest itself in your own life? What does it look like for you when you are afraid? What can you learn from David's battle plan for confronting his own fears?

Let's Pray

Father, this world is so full of trouble and often my fears assault me like an armed battalion. Help me learn how to fight the giant of fear with the weapons of faith. When I'm afraid, I put my trust in You, in God whose Word I praise, in God I trust, I will not be afraid. What can flesh do to me? You are my hope, my Shield, my Sword, my Protector, and my God. Please strengthen me with Your courage and grant me the victory in this fight of faith. In Jesus' mighty name I pray. Amen.

19 *God Changes Seasons*

GENESIS 8:22

"While the earth remains, seedtime and harvest, cold and heat, summer and winter, day and night, shall not cease."

Here's a promise for the struggling saint: God changes the seasons. Night *will* be followed by day and winter will be shadowed by spring and summer. If it has been a dark season in your soul, take heart. The leaves may have fallen, but that doesn't mean that the trees are dead. The fog may have descended and hidden the landscape, but that doesn't mean there isn't beauty and glory underneath. The sun will rise and once again heat your cold heart with its rays of love. The Lord of all seasons is faithful. Spring will arrive and you will see the light, feel the warmth upon your skin, and enjoy the gentle breeze on your neck.

God wants you to experience a renewed sense of hope today in His goodness for what is to come tomorrow. As long as the earth remains, seasons *will* change. New growth *will* come. And as seasons change, the steadfast love of the Lord will never cease and His mercies never come to an end. They are new every single morning, so great is His faithfulness (Lam. 3:23). With eager anticipation, you can look forward to your future, knowing that goodness and mercy will pursue you through every season until your eyes close on this earth and open to behold the glory of your faithful Lord in the new heavens and earth (Ps. 23:6).

God is faithful through summer and winter, and He is faithful through springtime and fall. Every instance the sun sets over the horizon and every occasion it peeks its head above the skyline is a proclamation of the faithfulness, mercy, and love of almighty God. As we experience natural blessings of the created order, material blessings of provisional grace, and spiritual blessings of peace with God and the presence of God with us, we can turn these mercies into moments of worshipful wonder and provocations to praise. The Lord of all controls all seasons, and He is gracious and kind.

Reflect

What season would you say your soul is in right now? What season would you like for your soul to be in at present? How does it comfort you to know that God is faithful and that He changes times and seasons?

Let's Pray

Lord, I thank You that You rule over the day and the night, the summer and the winter, the springtime and the harvest, the cold and the heat, the sunrise and the sunset. You are in complete control of the seasons of my life. Help me to look to You, trust in You, and embrace Your faithfulness in this present season I am in. You are sovereign, and You are good, and I love and trust in You. In Jesus' name, amen.

20 *Tell It to the Lord*

PSALM 34:15

The eyes of the LORD are toward the righteous and his ears toward their cry.

Friend, I don't know what you're going through at this exact moment, but I know somebody who would love to hear about it, someone whose eyes are ever on you for your good, someone whose ears are thoughtfully attending to your cries. Some of the best advice I've ever received in my entire life is contained in five words: "Tell it to the Lord." This invitation has the power to completely change our lives. Whatever it is you are wrestling with, whatever it is you're struggling with, whatever it is you're carrying, whatever it is you're burdened by, or whatever it is you're happy about ... for every type of emotion and every form of feeling you could have, the summons is to "Tell it to the Lord."

The Lord's ears are the most understanding that you have access to. He invites you to share everything with Him and He is never irritated by the fears or tears you bring to Him. He is able to sympathize with your every weakness, to weep when you weep, and to rejoice when you rejoice (Heb. 4:15). In communion with Him, your circumstances may not immediately change, but your heart will be changed by His presence.

The Lord wants to hear from you. Here is a friend who sticks closer than a brother (Prov. 18:24). He is a friend who empathizes with the poor of spirit, for He knows what it is like to walk this earth full of brokenness and broken hearts (John 11:35). As the old hymn proclaims, "What a friend we have in Jesus, all our sins and griefs to bear! What a privilege to carry everything to God in prayer!"[1] My friend, share your

---

1. Joseph Medlicott Scriven (1855). Public domain.

heart with your Lord. It is safe and wise and welcome for you to tell it to the Lord: "For the eyes of the LORD range throughout the earth to strengthen those whose hearts are fully committed to him" (2 Chron. 16:9 NIV).

Reflect

Is there anything you would be hesitant to share with the Lord? Does it help you to understand that He already knows everything you've gone through, everything you're thinking, and everything you've ever done? He invites you to commune with Him through prayer on anything and everything, and He will hear your cries.

Let's Pray

Father, I'm so grateful that Your eyes are constantly on me for my good and that You hear my prayers and all my cries for help. You say, "Call upon me in the day of trouble; I will deliver you, and you shall glorify me" (Ps. 50:15). I want to talk with You about every-thing, as someone would their best friend and closest ally. Thank You for the invitation and the encouragement to share my heart. [What do you need to tell the Lord? Will you tell Him?] My heart is Yours. In Jesus' name, amen.

21 *When You Feel Weak*

2 CORINTHIANS 4:7

But we have this treasure in jars of clay, to show that the surpassing power belongs to God and not to us.

If you wake up in the middle of the night and your mind races a million miles per hour and it's hard for you to stop it . . . if you wake up in the morning feeling overwhelmed . . . if when you get in your car and you have your first quiet moment of the day, it's like a faucet has been turned on and the water begins to flow out of the corners of your weary eyes . . . here's some tender encouragement for you in the midst of the craziness: "We have this treasure in jars of clay, to show that the surpassing power belongs to God and not to us."

There is a heavenly reason for our human weaknesses. God will have us, and all others in our lives, know that the power we have belongs to God and not to us. The power in us is purposefully packaged to promote the praise of God's glorious grace. The origin of any influence or impact we have is from above and not from us. So here's a proper response to our feelings of weakness: we submit, surrender, and serve.

Submit: "Submit yourselves therefore to God" (James 4:7). "Humble yourselves, therefore, under the mighty hand of God so that at the proper time he may exalt you, casting all your anxieties on him, because he cares for you" (1 Peter 5:6–7).

Surrender: As Jesus prayed on the Mount of Olives just before His arrest and crucifixion, so we pray, saying, "Father, if you are willing, remove this cup from me. Nevertheless, not my will, but yours, be done" (Luke 22:42).

Serve: A jar of clay was intended to hold precious treasure, to preserve its wealth, and to provide as a blessing for future generations. Jesus said,

"Whoever would be great among you must be your servant . . . even as the Son of Man came not to be served but to serve, and to give his life as a ransom for many" (Matt. 20:26–28).

Your weakness only serves to draw more attention to the greatness and glory of your Savior, and your life matters because of the inestimable treasure you hold in Him.

Reflect

Where do you feel your weaknesses most acutely? How does this meditation encourage you regarding those weaknesses you feel so deeply?

Let's Pray

Lord, thank You for showing me the heavenly reason for my human weaknesses. You will have me—and everyone in my life—know that the power in my life belongs to You and not to me. Your grace is sufficient for me, for Your power is made perfect in weakness. "Therefore, I will boast all the more gladly of my weaknesses, so that the power of Christ may rest upon me. For the sake of Christ, then, I am content with weaknesses, insults, hardships, persecutions, and calamities. For when I am weak, then I am strong" (2 Cor. 12:9–10). Thank You, Lord, for every weakness that reminds me that I have this treasure in jars of clay to show that this surpassing power belongs to You and not to me. Please be glorified in all my weaknesses. In Jesus' name, amen.

22　*When You Feel Anxious*

ISAIAH 35:3-4

*Strengthen the weak hands, and make firm the feeble knees.
Say to those who have an anxious heart, "Be strong; fear not!
Behold, your God will come . . . He will come and save you."*

The Lord of all has special support for fearful hearts. Whereas God lays low the pride of the ruthless (Isa. 13:11b), He purposes to come to the aid of the anxious, to strengthen them by His power, and to settle their trembling hearts in the glory of His presence. Here is God's heart for you anxious souls: "Be strong; fear not! Behold, your God will come . . . He will come and save you."

God is committed to rescue His own. That's why He sent Jesus from heaven to earth, and "the saying is trustworthy and deserving of full acceptance, that Christ Jesus came into the world to save sinners" (1 Tim. 1:15). Be strengthened by the certainty of God's eternal love for you. Your anxiety is an opportunity to see the power of God displayed on your behalf.

You can remind yourself that you are anxious because you care, and that your care is a beautiful thing because it means you love people, and you want to do what's right. Yet this care is also a burden: you feel its heaviness and that's hard for you. But your anxiety is not just a *burden*; it is also an *invitation*, and that invitation is for you to experience communion with the living God. God invites you, summons you, and beckons you to cast all your anxieties on Him because "he cares for you" (1 Peter 5:7). So, take heart, dear anxious believer. *You are not the only one who cares. God* cares for you. Cast all your cares *on the One who cares*, and He will help you carry those burdens.

What is burdening you right now? Is your heart weighed down with worries about your welfare? Fears about your future? Are you concerned with what kind of circumstances are lurking around the corner for you? Perhaps you're anxious about your relationship with a family member or a dear friend, or maybe it's the might of the mundane that rests heavy on your soul, or the longing for love, or the yearning for meaning and significance. Whatever burden you are bearing, bring it to the Lord and bless God for it: "Blessed be the Lord, who daily bears us up; God is our salvation" (Ps. 68:19). Praise God for the burdens that bring you back to Him! Bless God for the distress of soul or depression of spirit that drives you back in dependence to your Father above! Your worries are a welcome mat from Him. Bring it all to Him. Cast it all upon Him. He will come to your aid. He will come to save you and your anxious heart will be settled in the truth of God's everlasting love for you in Christ!

Reflect

Do you have an anxious heart right now? If so, what is God's encouragement to you as you meditate on these Scriptures?

Let's Pray

Father, search and know my heart and all my anxious thoughts. See if there is any grievous way in me and please lead me in the way everlasting. Thank You for the promise to come and save me. Lord, please strengthen my weak hands and make firm my feeble knees; please come to me and and save me, I pray. In Jesus' name, amen.

23 *Jesus Understands Your Pain*

ISAIAH 53:3

He was despised and rejected by men,
a man of sorrows and acquainted with grief.

Jesus was known as a man of sorrows, well acquainted with grief. Our Savior knew what it felt like to be scorned and mocked. He understood rejection. He encountered deep betrayal. He faced the loss of loved ones. He experienced exhaustion, sleepless nights, and deep sorrow.

Besides all of His own anguish, He carried the sorrow and suffering of those around Him. He welcomed with open arms the weary, the broken, the hurting, the diseased, the distressed, the disillusioned, and even those who had made a mess of their own lives by their own choices. That the "Man of Sorrows" would be called the "Friend of sinners" is a beacon of hope for everybody breathing in this broken world (see Luke 7:34).

Here's what it means: it means that *Jesus understands your pain*. He gets it. He can sympathize with you in your weaknesses. There's no sin or suffering that can surprise Him; He has gone before us in both pain and comfort. Now "as we share abundantly in Christ's sufferings, so through Christ we share abundantly in comfort too" (2 Cor. 1:5). So, we can go to Him, although trembling, and tell Him our trouble just as it is. He can handle it, He can understand it, and He can help us with it. He is the Great High Priest and He is able to sympathize with our weaknesses. He was tempted in every way but never once sinned. Because of this, we can come to the throne of grace and be met with mercy and grace in every time of need (see Heb. 4:14–16).

Take heart, dear child of God: the Man of Sorrows is the Friend of sinners.

Reflect

How does considering the sufferings of Jesus help you have fellowship with Jesus and strengthen you to persevere through your own suffering?

Let's Pray

Jesus, thank You for the fellowship of sharing in Your sufferings. Thank You that You understand all my pain and sorrow, and that You have called me Your friend. You were tempted in every way, yet without sin. As I draw near to the throne of grace right now, Lord, I pray that You would meet me with mercy and help me find all the grace I need for this time of need. In Your name I pray. Amen.

24   *Your Labor Is Not in Vain*

HEBREWS 6:10

For God is not unjust so as to overlook your work and the love that you have shown for his name in serving the saints, as you still do.

Cheer up, dear believer. Your labor is *not in vain*. It may feel for a time like your hard work is not making a difference, but you can rest assured that "in all toil there is profit" (Prov. 14:23) under the banner of a just God. God has not overlooked *anything* that you have done to serve other people for His glory. A comforting aspect of God's justice is that He takes note of our work and the love we show for others.

The Lord sees your work. He sees your love. He sees the time, effort, energy, and enthusiasm that you have exerted in attending to your family, your loved ones, your community, and your world. He takes note of all of that, and He will reward you for it. What does Jesus say in Matthew 10:42? "Whoever gives one of these little ones even a cup of cold water because he is a disciple, truly, I say to you, he will by no means lose his reward." He notices what you do and is planning how to reward you.

He does not overlook the love that you have shown for His name in serving the saints (past tense) as you still do (present tense). The almighty sovereign Lord of all is all-seeing and all-knowing. "Be steadfast, immovable, always abounding in the work of the Lord, knowing that in the Lord your labor is not in vain" (1 Cor. 15:58).

God has arranged life in His kingdom in such a way that we get the honor of doing the good works He has prepared for us and the joy of standing in amazement with our jaws dropped in wonder as we watch what only He can do through those good works. It's all by grace so He gets all the glory. Ephesians 2:8–10 says, "For by grace you have been saved through faith. And this is not your own doing; it is the gift of God, not a result of works, so that no one may boast. For we are his workmanship, created in Christ Jesus for good works, which God prepared beforehand, that we should walk in them."

So, don't give up. Don't become weary, but do good to all you can, and especially for your fellow believers (see Gal. 6:9–10).

Reflect

When have you felt like your love and your labors have gone unnoticed? What encouragement can we draw from the passages in this meditation?

Let's Pray

Father, thank You for the assurance that You see—and have seen—every sacrifice and labor of love that I have ever done in Your Name. You have prepared good works in advance for me to walk in, and You see, You know, and You reward me when I walk in those good works. Please fill me with the Holy Spirit and give me strength and energy to be steadfast, immovable, and always abounding in Your work, knowing that my labor for You is not in vain. In Jesus' precious name I pray. Amen.

25 Our Work and God's Work

MARK 4:26-29

And he said, "The kingdom of God is as if a man should scatter seed on the ground. He sleeps and rises night and day, and the seed sprouts and grows; he knows not how. The earth produces by itself, first the blade, then the ear, then the full grain in the ear. But when the grain is ripe, at once he puts in the sickle, because the harvest has come."

The passage above speaks of God's work and our work in the kingdom of God. Jesus likens the work of the kingdom to a farmer in a field. A farmer sows and scatters seed, and then he sleeps; all the while, God is at work in the earth to bring forth the fruit, to produce the crop. The farmer is to spread the seed extensively, trusting the Sovereign One exclusively. Seed may lie dormant for a long while, but that does not mean that nothing is happening in the field. God is in control of the rain and the temperature and the timing of any and all growth.

Jesus wants us to look at the fields and learn from the farmers that *this* is the way God's kingdom works. As Paul said, "I planted, Apollos watered, but God gave the growth. So neither he who plants nor he who waters is anything, but only God who gives the growth" (1 Cor. 3:6–7). God's kingdom grows often imperceptibly at first in the hearts of those with whom we've shared the Word. There is mystery here, as it takes just the right conditions to germinate the seed at just the right time for the seed to sprout and grow.

We cannot control all the conditions, but we can spread the seed and ask the Sovereign Lord to do what only He can do. Spreading and seeking is the way of the kingdom of God. So is sleeping . . .

Notice here that the farmer scatters seed *and then sleeps*. He has a job to do but is dependent on things outside of his control. It takes the right conditions to germinate the seed at the right time, and that's not something he can do by himself. This is like life in the kingdom of God.

When we partner with the Lord in His work, we get the joy of seeing what only God can do. After we have worked hard and prayed hard, let us sleep hard, looking to the Lord to bring the fruit that only He can bring. The farmer knows that:

Only God can bring the rain .. soften the soil . . . protect the seed . . . cause the seed to take root . . . safeguard the crop from destruction . . . make the harvest come because only God can give the growth . . . so only God gets all the glory.

The realization that God gets the glory does not make us stop working but invigorates our efforts. Let us go to bed every night with a smile on our face because our efforts matter to the King of the universe who can bring forth the fruit!

Reflect

Of these three actions, which is hardest for you: *spreading* seed for the kingdom of God, *seeking* the Lord for His blessing on your sowing, or *sleeping* in trust in the sovereign goodness of God to bless your efforts? Why is that action the hardest for you, and how does this meditation encourage you in that area?

Let's Pray

Father God, all my fruit is in You. You are the Sovereign One who gives all the growth, so You get all the glory. Lord, help me spread seed extensively while trusting You exclusively. Life in the kingdom of God is thrilling, and I pray that You would energize my efforts in serving You. Even as I sleep, I pray You would bless the seeds I have sown and bring forth a harvest of good fruit and righteousness. With joy, I will give You all the glory for what only You can do! In Jesus' mighty name I pray. Amen.

26   *Greatly Loved*

DANIEL 9:23

"At the beginning of your pleas for mercy a word went out, and I have come to tell it to you, for you are greatly loved."

Friend, do you think that an angel sent from heaven would address *you* with any less affection than the way Daniel is addressed as above? Do you suppose God Himself would speak to you with less comforting words? I don't. Oh, you who are in Christ, hear the Lord say that *you are greatly loved*!

Jesus said, "Greater love has no one than this, that someone lay down his life for his friends. . . . I have called you friends, for all that I have heard from my Father I have made known to you" (John 15:13–15). And elsewhere He has described Himself as the good shepherd who knows His flock well and is willing to give up His life for them (John 10:14–15).

Believer, you have every right to say with the apostle Paul, "I have been crucified with Christ. It is no longer I who live, but Christ who lives in me. And the life I now live in the flesh I live by faith in the Son of God, *who loved me and gave himself for me*" (Gal. 2:20).

Perhaps just now you may say, "Well, I'm not even sure I'm a Christian. How do I *know* that God loves *me*?" You know other believers who have found their joy in Christ, but Christ did not die for them alone. *You* were in His heart and on His mind as He bore the cross of Calvary. Look to Jesus and believe! "Everyone who calls on the name of the Lord will be saved" (Rom. 10:13). Everyone means every *one*. That includes you, dear reader! New believers and seasoned ones alike benefit from rereading John 3:16.

Believe that Jesus loves you and that He died for *you*. Turn to Him and hear Him say that *you are greatly loved*. If you don't sense God's affection for you, perhaps it is because you are looking in the wrong spot for proof of His love. If you look within, you will never find reason for Him to love you. Joy and peace will elude you if you look inside for evidence of God's love. His love for you has never been based on you or *your* performance. He loves you with an everlasting love (Jer. 31:3). Look to Christ and you will soak your heart in an ocean of love. Look to the crucified Savior and see how wide His outstretched hands are open for you. Look to Calvary and hear the cries of full and free forgiveness for every sinner who hides within the wounds of Jesus. Believer, *you are greatly loved*!

Jesus said, "Whoever comes to me I will never cast out" (John 6:37). Why not open your heart to Him right now and say, "Lord Jesus, I acknowledge that I am a sinner, but You came into the world to save sinners; please save me now in Your great love—I give myself to You. I am Yours. Amen."

God *will* receive you as you turn to Him, and He *will* shower you with His great love!

Reflect

Do you sense God's great affection for you? Where do you normally look for proof of God's love, and where is God calling you to look right now?

Let's Pray

Father, I thank You now that Your love for me is not based on my performance or anything within me. You showed Your love for me in that while I was still a sinner, Christ died for me (Rom. 5:8). Help me get my eyes off myself and onto Jesus, so that I may soak my heart in the ocean of Your love. By the power of Your Spirit, help me to hear from You in the deepest core of my being that I am greatly loved. I thank You, Father, for sending Your Son to live and die for me, that I might be reconciled to You and have the hope of eternal life. In Jesus' name I pray. Amen.

27 *Replenished*

"For I will satisfy the weary soul, and every languishing soul I will replenish."

Y ou and I were created in the image of God for communion with God and to reflect the glory of God. Our primary purpose here is *so vertical.* That's why temporary things like notoriety or money and possessions or security or intimacy within human relationships won't fully satisfy our desires and our deepest longings. Those are all *horizontal.*

We were created for the eternal. We were created for a relationship with God.

The good news is that God sent His Son, Jesus, to live the perfect life that we could never live, to die on the cross as a substitute, to receive the punishment that we deserve, and to rise from the grave defeating death and sin and Satan, so that we could be forgiven of our sins and given the gift of eternal life. And set free, ultimately, from the worthless pursuit of lesser glories so that our hearts will find their rest where they can only find their rest—in Jesus.

Jesus offers satisfaction to weary, thirsty, languishing souls. To the woman at the well He said, "Everyone who drinks of *this* water will be thirsty again, but whoever drinks of *the water that I will give him* will never be thirsty again. The water that I will give him will become in him a spring of water welling up to eternal life" (John 4:13–14). The woman He was speaking to had tried drinking deeply from the well of one human relationship after another, but nothing satisfied her. She had been intimate with at least six men, having had five prior husbands and then living with another man who was not her husband. Yet none of those men could quench her thirst. Her soul was weary. Jesus did not condemn her;

instead, He met her with true, eternal, everlasting love (see John 3:17). He offered her a drink from the only well that satisfies, the water He gives in Himself. Now Jesus offers to all of us, "If anyone thirsts, let him come to me and drink" (John 7:37). Perhaps you've tried every other well and come up empty. Drink now from the fountain of life. In His life, you will find life for your soul!

Reflect

Do you feel like you are languishing in your soul right now? How does it comfort and strengthen you to hear the Lord say, "I will satisfy the weary soul, and every languishing soul I will replenish"? Will you ask Him to replenish you now? "Taste and see that the LORD is good" (Ps. 34:8).

Let's Pray

Lord Jesus, thank You for offering true satisfaction to my weary, thirsty, languishing soul! I want to drink deeply of the water that You offer, and I pray that as I drink of Your water, it would become in me a spring, welling up to eternal life. Please replenish me, fill me with the Holy Spirit, and quench my thirsty soul. I am Yours completely. In Your name I pray, amen.

28 *Reassurance for Restless Souls*

1 SAMUEL 12:22

"For the LORD will not forsake his people, for his great name's sake, because it has pleased the LORD to make you a people for himself."

Think of this! God's name is at stake in what becomes of His people. Dear believer, God's name is at stake in what becomes of *you*. The reality of the irrefutable connection between God's own reputation and the immortal destiny of every one of His children should usher in remarkable reassurance to restless souls. Let all anxiety dissipate in the wondrous truth that God will not forsake you. He *cannot* forsake His own people and still be called faithful. Your eternal good and the worthiness of God's very character are shown to be united here in our text.

If left to yourself, you would surely fall away from Him, but that is not what we have here. You are not left to yourself. You are not on your own. You are under the Lord's great care and watchful eye, and He has promised to keep you to the end. Is this not tender mercy and glorious grace? "Consider what great things he has done for you" (1 Sam. 12:24).

Because God's glory and your good are bound together, He "will sustain you to the end, guiltless in the day of our Lord Jesus Christ. God is faithful, by whom you were called into the fellowship of his Son, Jesus Christ our Lord" (1 Cor. 1:8–9). God will keep you, support you, sustain you, strengthen you, empower you, and preserve you until the very end (see Ps. 121:5, 8).

God's pleasure rests on you, dear believer! Since He has promised to not forsake you, see to it that you do not forsake Him. Express your gratitude in a life full of worship and praise. In view of His mercy, offer every aspect of your life to Him, praying, "Lord, please bless the words of my mouth, the meditation of my heart, the work of my hands, and the path of my feet; please enable me to enrich the lives of all around me for Your glory, and please preserve me to the very end until my eyelids close in death and I awake to see Your face in glory!"

Reflect

Have you ever considered God's glory and your destiny to be woven together for all eternity?

Let's Pray

O Great God, how merciful You are! It has pleased You to make a people for Yourself, and it's my greatest joy to be one of Your children. Since what becomes of me now reflects on Your Name, I can trust You to take care of me. You are Almighty, merciful, gracious, and kind. Lord, please bring glory to Your name in continuing to hold me fast in faithfulness. In Jesus' name, amen.

29 *Under the Smile of God*

Therefore, since we have been justified by faith, we have peace with God through our Lord Jesus Christ. Through him we have also obtained access by faith into this grace in which we stand, and we rejoice in hope of the glory of God.

Believer, you have been *justified*! To be justified is to be declared righteous in the sight of God before the throne of God. This wonderful gift is bestowed upon all who believe in the Lord Jesus Christ and trust in Him for their salvation. "For by works of the law no human being will be justified in his sight" (Rom. 3:20); rather, we "are justified by his grace as a gift, through the redemption that is in Christ Jesus" (Rom. 3:24). In sending Jesus as our Savior, God did for us what we could never do for ourselves—namely, live a perfect, sinless life *in our place*. Jesus' righteousness has been credited to the believer's account. Now, it is "just-as-if-I'd" never sinned. That is remarkable mercy!

The good news doesn't end there. In our text above, we see two blessings that follow our justification. First, "we have *peace with God* through our Lord Jesus Christ." Though formerly in our unbelieving state we were at enmity with God, now through faith in Jesus we have been declared to be in a right state with God, and this results in *peace with God*. The peace referred to here is not a subjective peace, but an objective one. It's not the peace of *feeling* but the peace of *standing*. Every dispute you and I had with God has been settled in Jesus' life, death, and resurrection on our behalf. Jesus lived in our place, died in our place, and rose in our place to secure for us peace with God the Father. We no longer live under the fear of judgment and wrath. We live in the fixed reality that we have peace with the living God. Lord, let Your settled peace settle into my soul this day that You and I are on good terms, and I am living under the smile of God.

Second, we have "access by faith into this grace in which we stand." Because of our justification, you and I can draw near to God with the assurance that we have been granted admittance with the King of kings and Lord of lords. We are standing in grace, accepted in the beloved. What joy these thoughts bring to our souls, "and we rejoice in hope of the glory of God" (Rom. 5:2b)!

Reflect

Do you live as if you are at peace with God and have access to the grace of God?

Let's Pray

Precious Lord, to think that I have peace with God and access to God makes my heart want to leap for joy—I rejoice in the hope I have in You! Thank You for settling the heavenly hostility I brought upon our relationship through my many transgressions, and thank You for forgiving me for every one of them through faith in Jesus Christ. Now, I come boldly to Your throne of grace and ask for more grace to help me in my time of need. Father, flood my soul with grace upon grace for Your glory, I pray in Jesus' name, amen.

30 Out of Gas

Awesome is God from his sanctuary;
the God of Israel—he is the one who gives power and strength to his
people.

Have you ever been driving and completely run out of gas? I have. I was taking kids home after a youth group event with my van running dangerously low on fuel, and because I had promised my friends that I would have their older kids home at a certain time, I pushed the vehicle to the very limit. I knew the parents had another commitment to rush off to and they needed their older kids to watch their younger siblings when they would be gone. So I passed every gas station and coasted into their driveway safely in time. I had enough fuel in the tank to get to my friends' house and to exit their neighborhood, but not enough to make it to the gas station. Our van ceased to function, and my kids and I were left stranded on the side of a busy street. I felt like an idiot. Thankfully, I had my cellphone and I was able to call my wife, who came to our rescue with a gas can. After refueling, we made it home safe and sound, but the whole experience was very stressful.

Cars need fuel. Cellphones need charging. You and I need power from above, and God is the one who gives us power and strength. The book of Acts tells us that "the God who made the world and everything in it, being Lord of heaven and earth, does not live in temples made by man, nor is he served by human hands, as though he needed anything, *since he himself gives to all mankind life and breath and everything* [*else*]" (Acts 17:24–25). The everlasting God is the Creator of the ends of the earth, and He holds undiminishable power. He does not grow faint or weary. When we plug in to the Lord, we renew the strength of our souls.

He gives power to the faint,

    and to him who has no might he increases strength.

Even youths shall faint and be weary,

    and young men shall fall exhausted;

But they who wait for the LORD shall renew their strength;

    they shall mount up with wings like eagles;

they shall run and not be weary;

    they shall walk and not faint. (Isa. 40:29–31)

Do you feel like you're running out of gas in your soul? Do you feel exhausted? Tired? Weary? Weak? Fainthearted? Run-down? God is the one who gives power and strength to His people, and He is able to renew your strength. Ask Him for strength from above, and as He renews you, give Him the glory that He alone deserves. "You then, my child, be strengthened by the grace that is in Christ Jesus" (2 Tim. 2:1).

Reflect

Have you ever run out of energy for your daily tasks? Have you petered out from serving? What was the solution for you?

Let's Pray

Lord, please refuel me. Please renew my strength. Please give me more power, more energy, more grace, and more love. I want to plug my soul in to You and recharge. Grant me Your power from above, I pray. In Jesus' name, amen.

31 *Riches for All*

For there is no distinction . . . for the same Lord is Lord of all,
bestowing his riches on all who call on him.

God shows no favoritism but bestows His riches on *all* who call on Him. This is both a humbling reality (for any who feel exceptional) and a strong encouragement (for those who feel unexceptional). The Lord does not discriminate. "God shows no partiality" (Rom. 2:11; Gal. 2:6). The treasure we possess is one that has been imparted from above and received by faith, not earned or won by works, and it is available to everyone who calls on the name of the Lord!

God showed Peter that he should not call any person common or unclean. The account of how Peter was instructed to set aside his religious and cultural preferences is told in dramatic fashion in Acts 10. The principle he learned is in full force for us today. No child of God should "be puffed up in favor of one against another. For who sees anything different in you? What do you have that you did not receive?" (1 Cor. 4:6–7). The apostle Paul wrote to the Corinthians about Jesus being "both their Lord and ours" (1 Cor. 1:2).

All human boasting is excluded as every sinner is on equal footing at the base of the cross. "From now on, therefore, we regard no one according to the flesh. . . . if anyone is in Christ, he is a new creation. The old has passed away; behold, the new has come" (2 Cor. 5:16–17).

Calling upon the name of the Lord is the key to receiving blessings from above, and once we've received those blessings, we are not to boast in ourselves as if we've earned them; instead, we are to give all glory and honor and praise to the One who has bestowed those blessings upon us. We're also to *share* God's blessings with others. The heart of God is benevolent. His arms are open wide. That's why Jesus said if we ask, we will receive, and if we seek, we will find, and if we knock, the door will be open to us (see Luke 11:9–13). So let us not want for want of asking! Once we've received, let us not hold on to the treasure for ourselves alone but share it joyfully with others.

In 2 Kings 6–7, there's a story of the acts of four courageous lepers during a severe famine in Samaria. Faced with impending death from starvation or the threat of a merciless death from enemy armies in the camp of the Syrians, the four lepers decided to risk their lives and enter the Syrians' camp in search for food. To their utter amazement and astonishment, by an act of God's deliverance, they found the enemy camp had been completely abandoned, yet filled with food and drink. So they feasted their famished bodies on the sustenance and carried off the silver and gold. Then they said to one another, "This is a day of good news and that good news is meant to be shared." Rather than keeping the spoils all to themselves, they spread the good news with all others to enjoy. The Lord would bid us to do the same, as the riches of the Lord are for all to enjoy!

Reflect

Is there an individual or a type of person or group of people you have thought that God does not want to bestow His riches upon? How does this meditation change your view of the heart of God? How can it inform your prayers right now?

Let's Pray

Lord, You are eager to bless, bestowing Your riches on all who call upon You; so, I call upon You now. I pray for more light, more love, more insight, more understanding, more wisdom and grace to grasp who You are and what You have done for me in Jesus. Please give me more of You! Help me in turn bless others with Your riches. Amen.

32 *Attracting Favor*

ISAIAH 57:15

---

*"I dwell in the high and holy place, and also with him who is of
a contrite and lowly spirit, to revive the spirit of the lowly, and to
revive the heart of the contrite."*

Scripture records that Manasseh was a king of Judah who "did what
was evil in the sight of the LORD" (2 Chron. 33:2). It was written
of him that he "led Judah and the inhabitants of Jerusalem astray, to do
more evil than the nations whom the LORD destroyed before the people of Israel" (2 Chron. 33:9). Yet even Manasseh found favor in God's
sight when he humbled himself before the Lord: "And when he was in
distress, he entreated the favor of the LORD his God and humbled himself greatly before the God of his fathers. He prayed to him, and God
was moved by his entreaty and heard his plea and brought him again to
Jerusalem into his kingdom. Then Manasseh knew that the LORD was
God" (2 Chron. 33:12–13).

Perhaps you, like Manasseh, feel far off, plagued by your own iniquities and painfully aware of your own faults, failures, and frailties. Lift
your eyes to the faithfulness of God. God is so merciful that He is unfal-
teringly drawn toward a tender heart expressing marks of humility, such
that the vilest among us can move the heart of God by entreaty.

We cannot *earn* God's favor, but we can *attract* God's favor by a right
spirit before Him. The Lord says, "But this is the one to whom I will
look: he who is humble and contrite in spirit and trembles at my word"
(Isa. 66:2), and the psalmist exclaims, "A broken and contrite heart, O
God, you will not despise" (Ps. 51:17). If we humble ourselves before
the Lord, He will lift us up (1 Peter 5:6; James 4:10). Submission *to*

God and humility *before* God attract the favor *of* God. He revives the spirit of the lowly and the heart of the contrite.

Reflect

Is there any area in your life where you need to humble yourself before God and acknowledge your need for Him? What would it look like for you to take the next step with the Lord in this area?

Let's Pray

Lord, I know I cannot earn Your favor, but I do want to attract it. I humble myself and acknowledge my need for You and my desire to please and honor You. I submit myself to You wholly and completely, and I draw near to the Lover of my soul. Please look upon me with favor and grant me Your tender mercy, I pray. In Jesus' name, amen.

33   *The Attention of God*

Behold, the eye of the LORD is on those who fear him,
on those who hope in his steadfast love.

Nothing escapes God's notice; nothing is hidden from His watchful eye: "The LORD looks down from heaven; he sees all the children of man; from where he sits enthroned he looks out on all the inhabitants of the earth, he who fashions the hearts of them all and observes all their deeds" (Ps. 33:13–15). God's gaze is pervasive, permeating every corner of the earth.

As the sun rises from one end of the heavens and makes its circuit to the other end of them, and as nothing is hidden from its heat, so the eyes of the Lord range throughout the earth and He gives strong support to those who fear Him (Ps. 19:1–6; 2 Chron. 16:9). Ancient kings of Israel and Judah were notable for whether they did what was right in the eyes of the Lord, or whether they did what was evil (1 Kings 15:5, 11), since "the eyes of the LORD are in every place, keeping watch on the evil and the good" (Prov. 15:3). Truly, "no creature is hidden from his sight, but all are naked and exposed to the eyes of him to whom we must give account" (Heb. 4:13).

What a wonder it is, then, and a cause for ceaseless praise that the eye of the Lord would look with favor on those who fear Him, on those who hope in His steadfast love! "The eyes of the LORD are toward the righteous and his ears toward their cry" (Ps. 34:15). You may have to scramble to garner any attention from the distracted world around you, but the eye of the Lord is ever upon you for your good. Dear believer, God is watching over you; you can rest in the shadow of the Almighty. Under His wings, you will find refuge, and His faithfulness will be your guard and a wall around you (Ps. 91:1, 4). The sovereign ruler of heaven and earth is on your side as your protector. What, then, do you have to fear?

The LORD is on my side; I will not fear.
What can man do to me?
The LORD is on my side as my helper;
I shall look in triumph on those who hate me. (Ps. 118:6–7)

Reflect

What comforts, encourages, or strengthens you as you consider God is watching over you?

Let's Pray

Father, I praise You and thank You that Your eyes are upon me for my good. I rest under the protection of Your watchful eye. I pray that You would help me today. Please lead me not into temptation, but protect me from evil and harm, fill me with Your Holy Spirit, and work in me what is pleasing in Your sight. I pray this in Jesus' name. Amen.

34 *Pour It Out*

---

*Trust in him at all times, O people; pour out your heart before him;
God is a refuge for us.*

Here is a sweet invitation for our souls this day: *Trust in God*. Our confidence must not be in our circumstances, but in the Lord who rules and reigns over our circumstances and over every detail of our lives. God is to be the object of our soul's dependence. Not only are we invited to *trust in Him*, but we are exhorted to trust in Him *at all times*.

Every second is a holy moment because every instance is an occasion for fresh reliance upon the living God. Whatever we are wrestling with, whatever we are stressed by, whatever we are carrying, whatever is burdening us, whatever we are happy about, whatever we are rejoicing in, and whatever is causing us pain, we are invited to bring it *all* to the Lord Almighty. Trust *in* God is most clearly expressed through communion *with* God "at all times."

Isn't it encouraging to hear that God invites us to pour out our hearts before Him? We can come to God with *anything and everything* and lay it all before Him through open and honest prayer. In what manner should we do this? We should "rejoice always, pray without ceasing, give thanks in all circumstances" (1 Thess. 5:16–18). We can cast our burdens on Him; we can tell Him all our troubles; we can confess to Him all of our sins; we can express all our concerns; we can communicate all our cares; and we can pour out all the good and the bad stored up in our hearts to the One who can handle it all and who can help us.

God welcomes us to be real with Him. What a kindness! What a grace! This type of realness is the only way to fully express our trust in

Him. This truth makes prayer a joy. You and I are invited to converse with the Lord as you would your best of friends. What joys and victories, temptations and struggles, anxieties and difficulties are you facing today? Tell it all to the Lord in open and honest prayer and experience the comfort and peace that only God can give.

Reflect

Is there anything you would be hesitant sharing with God in prayer? If so, what's the hesitancy?

Let's Pray

Lord, thank You for the invitation to pour my heart out to You. I want to share with You the real state of my heart right now, not the "cleaned up" version—so here's how I'm really doing [honestly share your heart]; here's how I'm really feeling [honestly share the real state of your heart]; here's the good, the bad, and the ugly [articulate it]; here's what I need help with right now [request it]. Lord, I entrust all this to You, and I trust in You. You are my refuge. In Jesus' name, amen.

35   *Driven into His Arms*

PSALM 72:12-13

---

*For he delivers the needy when he calls, the poor and him who has
no helper.
He has pity on the weak and the needy, and saves the lives of the
needy.*

G od feels kindhearted compassion toward us in the consideration
of our neediness and sympathetic sorrow in the light of our distresses. His tender heart of mercy is moved with pity to comfort suffer-
ers and to save the destitute. When we come to Him with bare hands
and tortured hearts, He hears our cries, and each of us will find ourselves at times among the poor and needy.

Notably, only those who recognize their need for God will call out
for deliverance from God. That's why Jesus said, "Blessed are the poor
in spirit, for theirs is the kingdom of heaven" (Matt. 5:3). When every
other avenue for rescue is exhausted, desperate people look up to God.
The one who has no other helper looks for help from above. It's a blessed
trouble that guides the soul in God's direction, as He is eager to display
His power, provision, and benevolence on behalf of all the needy who
call upon Him. What a promise is held out for those who feel their need!
The Lord invites us with these generous words: "Call upon me in the
day of trouble; I will deliver you, and you shall glorify me" (Ps. 50:15).
In such a glorious provision, we get the deliverance, and the Lord gets
all the praise.

Dear reader, an inward sense of independence is not a blessing. It does
not lend itself toward communion with God, but to half-hearted religi-
osity, having the "appearance" of godliness but denying its power (see 2
Tim. 3:5). The Lord reproaches this kind of attitude of self-sufficiency

and pride: "I know your works: you are neither cold nor hot. Would that you were either cold or hot! So, because you are lukewarm, and neither hot nor cold, I will spit you out of my mouth. For you say, I am rich, I have prospered, and I need nothing, not realizing that you are wretched, pitiable, poor, blind, and naked" (Rev. 3:15–17).

If, on the other hand, today you feel your need, thank God for all your trouble! Thank the Lord for the hard stuff that drives you into His arms, because that's exactly where you belong.

Reflect

What's hard in your life right now? How may God want to use that hard stuff to draw you near?

Let's Pray

Lord, I need You. Apart from You, I am nothing and I have nothing. I am pitiable, poor, blind, and naked. I bring my neediness to Your endless supply of tender mercy and grace. Please deliver me, help me, have pity on me, and save me from my troubles today and for all eternity. I fling myself wholly and completely upon Your tender mercy. In Jesus' name, amen.

36 *Straining Forward*

PHILIPPIANS 3:13-15

But one thing I do: forgetting what lies behind and straining
forward to what lies ahead, I press on toward the goal for the prize
of the upward call of God in Christ Jesus. Let those of us who are
mature think this way.

Here is a Christ-centered, forward-focused, goal-driven, single-minded soul set on eternity with Jesus. Paul said, "Indeed, I count everything as loss because of the surpassing worth of knowing Christ Jesus my Lord" (Phil. 3:8). This was a man consumed with Christ. When living is Christ, then dying can only be gain (Phil. 1:21).

Does this passion describe the state of your own heart at present? Of my heart? If not, may God grant us grace to be captured with craving for Christ, so much so that everything else is worthless in comparison. May we seek the things above and set our minds on the things above, as is fitting for a child of God and heir of grace, as we are reminded of in Colossians 3:1–4.

This mindset is not something reserved for a *few* of God's people, but available for *all*. Our text above advised that those who are mature in the faith should strive for this attitude (Phil. 3:15). A mark of mature faith is a focus on future grace rather than being dragged down by the past, either our own failings or from difficulties common to our earthly life: "forgetting what lies behind." To be sure, the apostle Paul never fully forgot his past: "formerly I was a blasphemer, persecutor, and insolent opponent" (1 Tim. 1:13). A mark of maturity is not a denial of the past, but a decided disposition to not dwell on the past. Past sins, failures, mistakes, and defeats—or victories, for that matter—are not as central as future mercies that are in store for the believer in Christ. We learn from our past, but we dwell on our future with Christ—a future that is as secure as if it were already ours.

"Therefore, preparing your minds for action, and being sober-minded, set your hope *fully* on the grace that will be brought to you at the revelation of Jesus Christ" (1 Peter 1:13).

Reflect

Do you tend to dwell on the past? How does this meditation help you set your hope on the grace to come? How can you intentionally strain forward to what lies ahead?

Let's Pray

Lord, I set my heart and soul completely on You. I commit my past to You—the good, the bad, and the ugly of it all—and I refuse to dwell on what lies behind. Instead, I focus fully on what lies ahead. Thank You that my future is secure in Christ. With Christ as my life, all my future is gain. Preserve me, gracious Lord, until the day I behold You face to face in glory! In Jesus' name, amen.

37 *Comfort in Affliction*

2 CORINTHIANS 1:3-4

Blessed be the God and Father of our Lord Jesus Christ, the Father of mercies and God of all comfort, who comforts us in all our affliction, so that we may be able to comfort those who are in any affliction, with the comfort with which we ourselves are comforted by God.

There is nothing in Scripture that promises our difficulties disappear the moment we trust in Jesus. Quite the opposite. Jesus likened discipleship to preparation for crucifixion (Matt. 16:24). The apostle Peter wrote, "Beloved, do not be surprised at the fiery trial when it comes upon you to test you, as though something strange were happening to you. But rejoice insofar as you share Christ's sufferings, that you may also rejoice and be glad when his glory is revealed" (1 Peter 4:12–13).

Paul stated that we are not to be thrown off course by our afflictions, because "you yourselves know that we are destined for this" (1 Thess. 3:3). A believer in Christ is destined for afflictions in this life. If you are bearing up under the weight of your suffering, it is not an indication of the absence of God. The trouble you are enduring is not an expression of a lack of God's love. No, the fact is, "to this you have been called, because Christ also suffered for you, leaving you an example, so that you might follow in his steps" (1 Peter 2:21). Just as we are destined for afflictions, so we are *destined for comfort* in all of our afflictions from the Father of mercies and the God of all comfort, as we read above.

A child most fully feels the comfort of a mother when, as the child is hurting, she is embraced in her mother's arms. So, too, God would have you experience the fullness of His love as you fall into His arms in your pain. Not only are we destined for afflictions in this life and destined for comfort amid our agony, but we are also *destined for glory* in the life to come:

> So we do not lose heart. Though our outer self is wasting away, our inner self is being renewed day by day. For this light momentary affliction is preparing for us an eternal weight of glory beyond all comparison, as we look not to the things that are seen but to the things that are unseen. For the things that are seen are transient, but the things that are unseen are eternal. (2 Cor. 4:16–18)

Bless God for His comforting mercies! Fall into His arms and enfold yourself in His loving hold on you. The day will come when God will turn your present troubles into blessings of comfort for others, as you comfort the hurting with the comfort with which you have been comforted by your heavenly Father.

Reflect

Where have you experienced God's comfort and love amid your afflictions? When have you comforted someone else?

Let's Pray

Father, I cast myself into Your comforting arms. You know my trials. They are not hidden from You. Please console me. Thank You that the day is coming when there will be no tears, no sorrow, no trouble, and no more suffering. I long for that day, but mainly I long for You. Comfort me now, and then use me to comfort others for Your glory. In Jesus' name, amen.

38 *When You Don't Feel Up for It*

PSALM 126:5

Those who sow in tears shall reap with shouts of joy!

Perhaps you've been laboring under the weight of a broken heart. You're in a season of sadness and the work never ceases until your eyelids close in weary sleep; then you arise the next morning just to start the process all over again. Dear reader, if that's you, don't be surprised as tears flow easily from your exhausted eyes.

Earlier on in our marriage, as our children were little, my wife worked so hard as a schoolteacher, nurse, counselor, mediator, chauffeur, entertainer, homemaker, housekeeper, cook, photographer, interior designer, and therapist (to me) all on a daily, repetitive basis! She didn't have the benefit of getting paid a market rate for all that labor, and the work never ended. These days, our kids are older, and the challenges are different—we're exhausted by 8:30 p.m. and that's usually when teenagers want to talk. The truth is the same in every season: God has arranged life to typically follow a pattern of sowing and reaping (2 Cor. 9:6; Gal. 6:7–9), and often there is work to be done when we don't feel up for it.

What do we do in those moments? We ask God for grace to serve in the strength that He provides, and then we sow, even while the tears fall (1 Peter 4:11).

Some weeks, we'll see a lot of fruit from our labors. Other weeks, we won't. I suppose it's like that with any type of work or profession. That's why some of the most encouraging truths in Scripture are the verse from Psalm 126 above and also "In all toil there is profit" (Prov. 14:23). Your tearful toil *will* be rewarded. You may not see it all today, but shouts of joy *will* come. So don't lose heart. Don't give up. Don't believe the lie that it's all for nothing. God sees, God knows, and God will reward those who sow in tears while trusting Him.

> Cast your bread upon the waters, for you will find it after many days. . . . In the morning sow your seed, and at evening withhold not your hand, for you do not know which will prosper, this or that, or whether both alike will be good. (Eccl. 11:1, 6)

Reflect

Do you have any work in front of you that you don't feel emotionally up for at present? What would it look like for you to sow in tears?

Let's Pray

Father, please give me grace to serve in the strength that You provide, so that in all things You may be glorified through Jesus Christ. Please grant me wisdom and energy, and please preserve me; as I sow in tears, fill me with hope that I will reap in shouts of joy for Your glory! In Jesus' name, amen.

39 *The Greatest Display of Strength*

PSALM 103:10

He does not deal with us according to our sins, nor repay us according to our iniquities.

O n a writing retreat in south Florida, I learned of a man who had an altercation with another individual on the streets of Miami. They exchanged punches and one of the men fell to the ground. Rising and dusting himself off, he left the scene and returned to his vehicle, apparently having lost the fight. That's when anger took control; in a fit of rage, he aimed his new Corvette at full speed onto the sidewalk, running over the individual who had struck him. When police arrived, they arrested the man for attempted vehicular homicide, while an ambulance took the injured pedestrian to the emergency room for treatment. Was this a display of strength? No, the whole scene was a spectacle of horror.

In contrast to this, God shows His power in the demonstrations of His patience. An ancient proverb says, "Whoever is slow to anger is better than the mighty, and he who rules his spirit than he who takes a city" (Prov. 16:32). Anyone can lose their temper, but it takes something stronger than might to keep the spirit in a tight rein. It takes the presence and power of the Almighty. The greatest display of strength is tenderness in the midst of provocation. Gentleness is the primo expression of power because the ruling of one's spirit is strength under control.

Jesus was the gentlest person to ever live on the face of this earth. On the cross, He prayed for His enemies who were crucifying Him: "Father, forgive them, for they know not what they do" (Luke 23:34). Now, Jesus invites us into His gentleness: "Come to me, all who labor and are heavy laden, and I will give you rest. Take my yoke upon you, and learn from me, for I am gentle and lowly in heart, and you will find rest for your souls" (Matt. 11:28–29).

We live in a world full of rage, and it is not a world full of rest. Rest and rage cannot coexist like gentleness and rest can. God is all powerful, and in His almighty power, He does not deal with us according to our sins, nor repay us according to our iniquities. This is good news for every offender. Let's rest in this mercy and learn to extend it to others with tenderness and strength.

> My sin—oh, the bliss of this glorious thought!—
> My sin, not in part but the whole,
> Is nailed to the cross, and I bear it no more,
> Praise the Lord, praise the Lord, O my soul![2]

Reflect

Where have you seen gentle strength on display?

Let's Pray

Almighty God, I praise You for Your strength and Your tenderness even in the midst of provocation. There is no one like You, slow to anger and abounding in steadfast love. Please fill my heart with Your tender mercy and strength to show Your gentleness in a world so full of rage. In Jesus' name, amen.

2. "It Is Well with My Soul," verse 3, Horatio Spafford (1873). Public domain.

40   *When God Is on Your Side*

PSALM 118:6-7

The LORD is on my side; I will not fear. What can man do to me?
The LORD is on my side as my helper; I shall look in triumph on
those who hate me.

The psalmist here meditates on the incredible benefits of having the Lord as his ally. First, he enjoys *relief from fear because the Lord is on his side*. What comfort, peace, and security that brings! Our flesh wages its war internally in our souls, the world is arrayed against us at every turn, and the devil seeks our ruin, but the bottom line is, "If God is for us, who can be against us?" (Rom. 8:31).

No one and nothing is greater than God, so it's a wonder of wonders that a sterling benefit of being a recipient of the gospel of grace is that *God* is now for us. God's omnipotence, omnipresence, omniscience, perfect wisdom, unconditional love, and comprehensive sovereignty is fully engaged toward the aid of those who trust in Him, so the assistance of God carries with it freedom from fear. Amazing. Breathtaking. Liberating. Let's all just take a deep breath and enjoy the relief.

Second, the psalmist glories in *the presence of the Lord as his help*. Incredibly, the Lord who was once our adversary is now our helper. With our sins forgiven in Christ, God is now favorably disposed to us. His inclination is to provide for us, to protect us, and to prosper our souls.

Like many of you, I have a strong personal friend who is wired as a defender. I believe God designs everyone uniquely, and He's designed this friend with a high degree of natural boldness and ability to get things done. Over the years, this friend has proven to be a persuasive, resilient, and influential force in my life for good. I whispered something to my wife recently as I witnessed him in action. I said, "I sure am glad he's on our side." Honestly, I would not want to be on the other side of his strength. If you have a companion like this, you know how good it is for a tough and capable supporter to be on your side. Think of it: *The Lord is on our side*. What more could we need?

Finally, the psalmist pronounces the *assurance of victory*: "I shall look in triumph on those who hate me." This is a strong encouragement to all of us who trust in the Lord. The day is coming when the Lord God Almighty will right every wrong, wipe every tear, remove every burden, and crush every crumb of opposition. We *shall* stand in triumph—the triumph of the risen Lamb (Rev. 21:3–4). Relief from fear. The presence of help. Assurance of victory. This is what it looks like to have the tender mercy of God Almighty on our side.

Reflect

Who is the strongest friend or ally you have ever had on your side? How does it encourage you to think of *God* being on your side as *your helper*?

Let's Pray

Lord, I thank You that You are Almighty, the Creator of the heavens and the earth and the Sustainer of all, and I thank You that You are with me and on my side. It blows me away to think of this. Please help me live in faith in Your power and Your promises. In Jesus' name, amen.

41   *Unending Mercies*

MATTHEW 13:12

*For to the one who has, more will be given, and he will have an
abundance.*

Could it be that the spring once opened to us will never run dry
(John 7:37–38)? Could it be that once we have received admittance and access to the throne of grace, our formerly trembling hearts
can now anticipate nothing but increasing glories (Heb. 4:16)? Could
it be that once we have tasted and seen that the Lord is good, blessing
upon blessing is sure to follow (Pss. 23:6; 34:8–10)? This is what Jesus
shares with His disciples in Matthew 13:12 above.

A child received into a loving family will be provided with food,
clothing, shelter, warmth, opportunities, instruction, care, attention,
safety, belonging, love, and a myriad of other blessings, for to the one
who has, *more will be given, and he will have an abundance.* Dear believer,
having received the glorious gift of salvation, do you now doubt your
heavenly Father's ongoing provision?

Oh, my soul, put every doubt to bed. "He who did not spare his own
Son but gave him up for us all, how will he not also with him graciously
give us all things?" (Rom. 8:32). Jesus is not ashamed to call us brothers
and sisters (Heb. 2:11), so let us not be bashful in embracing our identity
as children of God. "See what kind of love the Father has given to us, that
we should be called children of God; and so we are" (1 John 3:1).

Have you been justified by His grace? Then, expect to be sanctified
as well. Being sanctified, expect to be glorified (Rom. 8:30) because "to
the one who has, more will be given."

Has God ever shown mercy to you? If so, you can expect more of
the same. His mercies "are new every morning" (Lam. 3:23). Christ will

distinguish His own. It is to the Father's glory that you bear much fruit, showing yourselves to be His disciples (John 15:8). You who have been given mercy, will be given more mercy! Let His past mercies foster your faith for future mercies and may you rest secure in your heavenly Father's love.

Reflect

When it comes to your relationship with God, do you think you have a scarcity mindset or a mindset of abundance?

Let's Pray

Father, there is nothing I have that I have not received from You. You have given me life, You have given me breath, You have given me everything else, including the gift of a relationship with You through Jesus. Forgive my hard thoughts and my unbelief and help me see how deeply You love me. Since You have given me grace in Jesus, please shower it upon me all the more! In Christ's name I pray. Amen.

42   Distress, Dread, and Our Deliverer

GENESIS 32:12

But you said, "I will surely do you good."

In this verse above, Jacob is reminding God of His promise to do good to him. This is such a wonderful display of humility and faith amid an occasion of fear, and every believer has much to learn from this prayer of Jacob.

Are you familiar with the story of Jacob and Esau? Here's a brief recap:

Jacob and Esau were twin brothers. Esau was the older and Jacob the younger. Through a course of unfortunate events for Esau, Jacob took his brother's birthright and also deceived their father, Isaac, into giving him the blessing that was intended for Esau as the firstborn. Esau decided that he was going to kill Jacob after their father died. So Jacob fled from the fury of his older brother and for twenty years, he took refuge with his uncle Laban. It had been twenty years since he had last seen his older brother when, obeying the command of the Lord, Jacob left Laban and at last is about to encounter his brother, Esau. Messengers arrive to Jacob's camp with this news: "We came to your brother Esau, and he is coming to meet you, and there are four hundred men with him" (Gen. 32:6).

Can you imagine the fear Jacob is experiencing as he is preparing to meet his estranged brother who is now accompanied by four hundred men? This is essentially an army moving toward Jacob, who knows his brother has hated him for taking away his birthright and blessing and who has previously planned to take his life. What is Jacob to do?

He responds with humble, desperate prayer to the God of tender mercy. Jacob's prayer acknowledges his own unworthiness and puts all his confidence in God's word and His covenant promises (see his prayer in Gen. 32:9–12). In answer to prayer, God mercifully softens Esau's heart, delivers Jacob, and restores the relationship of these two estranged brothers (Gen. 33). This is amazing grace!

Let me learn in my fear to turn to God for mercy. I, too, must acknowledge my own unworthiness and take all my dread to the one who can deliver. May I lay my distress before my Deliverer with comparable humility and trembling faith and exclaim: "But you said, 'I will surely do you good,'" and You have offered for me to "call upon me in the day of trouble; I will deliver you, and you shall glorify me" (Ps. 50:15).

Reflect

What promises *from* God would you like to take back *to* God, just as Jacob prayed, "But you said, 'I will surely do you good'"?

Let's Pray

Father, I agree with Jacob that I am not worthy of the least of all the kindnesses You have shown to me, but You have said, "I will surely do you good." So, I cast my cares and my fears on You and pray that You would honor Your word and show me Your goodness as You showed Your goodness to Jacob. In Jesus' mighty name I pray. Amen.

43   *The Reason Jesus Came*

MATTHEW 9:12-13

He (Jesus) said, "Those who are well have no need of a physician, but those who are sick. Go and learn what this means: 'I desire mercy, and not sacrifice.' For I came not to call the righteous, but sinners."

J esus reveals Himself here as the merciful Physician of our souls. Just as a physician must enter the world of the sick *to heal anyone's body*, so the Son of Man eats and drinks with sinners precisely *because they need a Savior*. Wouldn't it be absurd for a physician to go through all the training, education, and preparation for his or her practice, only to stay away from anyone who could benefit from that expertise and care? No doubt there are doctors who become experts in their field because of the financial benefits and esteem of their position, but many do so out of compassion and the desire to extend mercy.

Jesus says here, "I desire mercy." Had He come to call the righteous, I would have never been called. Had He come for the healthy, I would have never heard His voice say, "Follow Me." Praise God that Jesus did not come for the healthy, but for the sick! Do you feel sick in your soul right now? If so, take heart—Jesus calls *you*. If Jesus had come for the righteous, *no one* would be called, for "none is righteous, no, not one" (Rom. 3:10). Why, then, does Jesus say, "I came *not* to call the righteous" when there is no one righteous (but Him)? The context of this passage offers us insight.

Jesus was speaking here to the Pharisees who trusted in their own adherence to the law for their righteousness before God, and they were blind to the depth of their own depravity. In other words, they did not see their need for a Savior. Those who think they are already righteous will not recognize the glory of Jesus even if He is standing in front of them. So God first shows us the brokenness of our hearts before He mends our souls.

As the heavenly Physician, Jesus holds an accurate diagnosis for our disease—*sin against a holy God*. He also carries the proper prognosis for that sin: eternal separation from God. But, mercifully and wonderfully, He provides the only cure—trust in the perfect life, substitutionary death, and glorious resurrection of the Son of God (Jesus) for the forgiveness of sins and the gift of eternal life. May we say with Paul,

> Christ Jesus came into the world to save sinners, of whom I am the foremost. But I received mercy for this reason, that in me, as the foremost, Jesus Christ might display his perfect patience as an example to those who were to believe in him for eternal life. To the King of the ages, immortal, invisible, the only God, be honor and glory forever and ever. Amen. (1 Tim. 1:15–17)

Reflect

What comfort does it bring you to hear Jesus say that He desires mercy, and where do *you* need mercy?

Let's Pray

Lord Jesus, thank You for being the Great Physician of souls. Thank You for coming from heaven to earth, not to call the "righteous" (or those who think they are already righteous) but to call sinners to Yourself. I recognize that I'm a sinner, and I'm so drawn to You. I accept Your call with gratefulness and joy. Amen.

44   *A Very Present Help in Trouble*

PSALM 56:9-11

This I know, that God is for me.
In God, whose word I praise, in the LORD, whose word I praise,
in God I trust; I shall not be afraid. What can man do to me?

God has spoken enough promises in His Word to silence the accusations of ten thousand tongues—even ten thousand times ten thousand tongues! What He has promised, He will be sure to fulfill though every person on earth and every demon in hell would stand against Him. Psalm 56 is a psalm of David under great duress as the Philistines seized him in Gath. See the enemies arrayed against him at every turn:

> "man tramples on me" (v. 1)
> "all day long an attacker oppresses me" (v. 1b)
> "my enemies trample on me all day long" (v. 2)
> "many attack me proudly" (v. 2b)
> "all day long they injure my cause" (v. 5)
> "all their thoughts are against me for evil" (v. 5b)
> "they stir up strife, they lurk" (v. 6)
> "they watch my steps, as they have waited for my life" (v. 6b)

Yet David makes this remarkable statement amid unimaginable opposition: "This I know, that God is for me." What extraordinary confidence in the tender heart of God is on display by David here! To what can we attribute such unshakable hope? How did David *know* that God was for him? Because of the promises of God: "In God, whose word I praise, in

God I trust; I shall not be afraid. What can flesh do to me?" (Ps. 56:4).

Perhaps you feel attacked, oppressed, trampled, and injured without cause. If so, lift your eyes to the Lord on high. Believer, the Almighty God of heaven and earth has spoken very great and tender things over your life, such that even death itself cannot separate you from His love (Rom. 8:31–39). What else matters in life than knowing that God is for us?

What more assurance do we need than this truth? Let's follow David's example and settle our hearts in the truth that God is indeed *for us*. As another psalmist sings, "God is our refuge and strength, a very present help in trouble. Therefore we will not fear though the earth gives way, though the mountains be moved into the heart of the sea, though its waters roar and foam, though the mountains tremble at its swelling" (Ps. 46:1–3)

Reflect

What's troubling you right now and tempting you to fear? Do you believe God is for you in the midst of it all?

Let's Pray

Father, You are my refuge. I thank You that You are with me and You are for me. I hide myself in You and pray that You would please calm my fears, strengthen my soul, steady my knees, and fill me with the Holy Spirit so I trust in You. In Jesus' name, amen.

45 *Who Salvation Belongs To*

ROMANS 9:16

So then it depends not on human will or exertion, but on God, who has mercy.

Salvation *belongs* to God (Ps. 3:8; Jonah 2:9; Rev. 7:10). When something belongs to you, it is yours to do with as you desire. Since salvation belongs to God, it is His to do with as He desires. So it does not depend on human desire or effort, but on God, who has mercy (Rom. 9:16). Dear reader, if you are not saved, what you need is not something that can be *earned* through human effort or exertion; it is something that can only be *received* by God's own mercy.

The good news is that "the LORD is merciful" (Ps. 103:8). First Timothy 2:3–4 reminds us that He desires "all people to be saved" and to know His truth. Further, "the Lord is not slow to fulfill his promise as some count slowness, but is patient toward you, not wishing that any should perish, but that all should reach repentance" (2 Peter 3:9).

God desires to give you the gift of salvation. Only the mercy of God can save us from the wrath of God. This realization should inspire holy fear, invoke sacred reverence, arouse awe, and awaken prayerful dependence on the Lord who is merciful.

Nehemiah describes God as one who is "ready to forgive, gracious and merciful, slow to anger and abounding in steadfast love" (Neh. 9:17c). God is ready to forgive *you*. Are you ready to receive His forgiveness and the gift of salvation? Just as no one who has ever experienced salvation has deserved it or earned it, so there is no distinction that can disqualify you from receiving it. Romans 10:12–13 assures us that everyone who calls on His name will be saved.

Call on the name of the Lord Jesus, and you, too, will be saved!

Reflect

Have you asked God for mercy? Have you turned from your sins and trusted in Jesus, the Savior, for forgiveness and for the gift of eternal life? If not, what is holding you back from requesting and receiving God's mercy?

Let's Pray

Lord, salvation belongs to You. I acknowledge that it does not depend on my will or my works or my efforts, but on Your mercy. Thank You, Lord, that You are a God who is gracious and merciful, slow to anger, and abounding in steadfast love. Please have mercy on me and save me, O Lord, I pray. Make me Yours—completely and eternally Yours. I surrender. Amen.

46 *Nevertheless*

Nevertheless, I am continually with you; you hold my right hand.
You guide me with your counsel,
and afterward you will receive me to glory.

Never-the-less. What an ocean of tender mercy and magnificent grace is found in this one word. Let us soak our souls in its goodness and relish every gentle wave it brings.

The author, Asaph, explains in this psalm how he was previously embittered in his soul, envying the prosperity of the wicked, and doubting God's goodness, sovereignty, and wisdom. Being wise in his own eyes, the psalmist was acting arrogantly toward the Lord, complaining in the bitterness of his soul, and doubting God's care, compassion, and control. God, in His mercy, opened Asaph's heart and mind as he sought the Lord in the sanctuary, and God enabled Asaph to see his circumstances from an eternal perspective. That's when everything changed internally for Asaph and he was convicted of his pride and arrogance, unbelief, and complaint. Asaph goes so far as to say,

> When my soul was embittered,
>   when I was pricked in heart,
> I was brutish and ignorant;
>   I was like a beast toward you. (Ps. 73:21–22)

That's when we arrive at the glorious word for our day's meditation: nevertheless. Yes, Asaph had doubted God's love. He had questioned God's care. He had mistrusted God's wisdom. He had distrusted God's goodness. He had disbelieved God's power. He had complained. He had considered that he could do a better job ruling the universe than God Himself. What an offense toward God.

Never-the-less. What four things does Asaph declare "nevertheless" about in the passage at the beginning of today's meditation? As you review these, make them your affirmation also.

Dearest believer, God's love meets you right where you are. In the midst of all your questions and doubts, hear the Lord say to you, "Nevertheless, I am with you." What a word! What a truth! What a Savior!

He has said, "I will never leave you nor forsake you." So we can confidently say, "The Lord is my helper; I will not fear; what can man do to me?" (Heb. 13:5–6).

Reflect

Where have you felt like you've blown it and yet heard the word "nevertheless" from God above? Isn't God's "nevertheless" amazing?!

Let's Pray

Lord God, You are so gracious, so merciful, so tender, so kind. Countless times I've been embittered in soul and instead of confronting me with judgment, You've met me with mercy. I'm so grateful, and I love You, Lord. Thank You for being with me continually through it all. In Jesus' name, amen.

47 *Sustained in Every Season*

PSALM 74:16-17

Yours is the day, yours also the night;
you have established the heavenly lights and the sun.
You have fixed all the boundaries of the earth;
you have made summer and winter.

Let us learn from the natural order of creation that *all* our seasons belong to God. Many who first trust in Christ begin their journey with the Lord full of vigor, joy, and zeal, as if there should be nothing but blue skies and clear sun shining across a full horizon until the moment of their final breath. Enjoying perhaps a lengthy period of the blissful smile of God, they become disillusioned when the clouds arise and the cold sets in.

Yet those of God's people who bear the scars of many rivers crossed and many seasons sustained are greatly comforted by the truth that the Lord who made summer has also made the winter. In the dark night of the soul, it is a tender mercy to be able to commune with God by affirming that "yours is the day, yours also the night." When mystified by what matches the sensations of an endless winter, it does one good to affirm to the Lord that "you have made summer *and winter.*"

May our aim be all of life lived in consecration to the God of every season. Every minute, every moment, every season, every second has been claimed by God.

If it is winter now in your soul, take heart. The presence of winter in your soul does not mean the absence of God in your life. Acknowledge His sovereignty. Humble yourself under the mighty hand of God, that He may lift you up in due time, and cast all your anxiety on Him because He cares for you (1 Peter 5:6–7). Pray for strength to endure the heavy blasts of cold. Your faith is being tested, and the testing of your faith will produce steadfastness (James 1:3). You will be stronger in your faith because of this season of endurance.

Pray also that your season of winter will end, and that springtime and summer will follow in your soul. Daniel blessed the God of heaven, proclaiming that "He changes times and seasons" (Dan. 2:21). What a word of hope for those in a season of sorrow! The boundaries of the earth have been fixed by God's command, and so have the borders of your present season. Until then, heed these words penned by James Procter, a onetime atheist who, during a serious illness, desperately reached out to Christ: "My soul is night, my heart is steel—I cannot see, I cannot feel; for light, for life, I must appeal in simple faith to Jesus."[3]

Reflect

What season of soul are you in at present? How can you take your present season to the Lord?

Let's Pray

Father, I thank You that all my times are in Your hand and that You rule over every season of my life. So, I acknowledge You as Lord of all my seasons, including this present season. Please uphold me, preserve me, sustain me in this season and in every season for Your glory. In Jesus' name, amen.

3. "A Hopeless Case?," Grace Bible Fellowship Church, March 30, 2017, https://gracebfcreading .org/a-hopeless-case/.

48 *The Rearview Mirror*

PHILIPPIANS 3:13-14

But one thing I do: forgetting what lies behind and straining forward to what lies ahead, I press on toward the goal for the prize of the upward call of God in Christ Jesus.

Have you ever considered that the windshield of a vehicle is much bigger than the rearview mirror? I think there's something for us to consider in that reality, some helpful insight into wisdom for life. There's also a lot of tender comfort here.

Each of us is on a journey. We are moving toward eternity, and every believer is *heading to glory*. God has not called us to go in reverse. He is calling us to press on toward the goal for the prize of the *upward* call of God in Christ. In other words, He is calling us home.

If a driver constantly stared in the rearview mirror while in motion, that driver would eventually crash! For perspective, we glance in the rearview mirror to get our bearings, but we're to keep our eyes *ahead* of us while in motion. The same should be true for every believer, every pilgrim on the journey toward the Celestial City. If you are tempted with the thought that your best days are behind you, you are staring in the rearview mirror with a sense of loss for what is gone. This is not a wise way to travel in this life: "Say not, 'Why were the former days better than these?' For it is not from wisdom that you ask this" (Eccl. 7:10). The Lord would encourage you that He has incredible things in store for your future, beauty and glory the likes of which this world could never know (1 Cor. 2:9)! So keep your eyes ahead of you and press on toward the goal of knowing the Lord.

Perhaps, on the other hand, you are tempted to look back at former days with a heart full of regret. If that is you, may the Lord comfort you with the reminder that all who are in Christ are fully, freely, and forever *forgiven*: "For I delivered to you as of first importance what I also received: that Christ died for our sins" (1 Cor. 15:3). Keep your eyes ahead of you and look with anticipation through the windshield of your life. Though you feel yourself unworthy, you *will* see vistas of glory that will take your very breath away. Grace and glory are in front of you for all eternity.

Reflect

What emotions surface for you when you think of your past? How does this meditation encourage you as you consider your future?

Let's Pray

Father, thank You for Your promises of a bright and glorious future. You have said, "For I know the plans I have for you, declares the LORD, plans for welfare and not for evil, to give you a future and a hope" (Jer. 29:11). I long for the day when I will see You face to face, and I will be fully redeemed and filled with joy in Your presence for all eternity. Until then, please give me wisdom as I continue to strain forward to what lies ahead, for Your glory. In Jesus' name, amen.

49 *The Tender Mercy of God's Watchful Eye*

PSALM 33:18-19

Behold, the eye of the LORD is on those who fear him,
on those who hope in his steadfast love,
that he may deliver their soul from death
and keep them alive in famine.

I've got my eye on you" is a phrase that can mean many different things. Depending on the context, it could be said in jest or taken as an expression of concern regarding another's motives or actions. In another setting, "I've got my eye on you" could be a warm gesture of romantic intent, as a husband may say playfully to his wife. Still in other instances, we may mean this statement in a protective sense, as in an appeal from a parent to an older sibling to "keep your eye on your brother" while the parent is away.

It's in this protective and caring way that God has His eyes on His people, for their good. The eye of the Lord is *protectively* upon those who fear Him even, as above, delivering their soul from death and keeping them alive in famine. First Kings 17:2–6 tells how the Lord made a way to provide for Elijah even when the waters ran dry.

As God took care of him during drought, so He will care for you who fear Him. What attracts God's attention and solicits His favor is the fear of the Lord. The eye of the Lord and the favor of God is upon those who fear Him, and those who fear Him can be recognized by their hope in His steadfast love because to fear Him is to hope in Him. To have the eye of the Lord upon you affectionately and protectively is a tender mercy.

He will command his angels concerning you
   to guard you in all your ways.
On their hands they will bear you up,
   lest you strike your foot against a stone.
You will tread on the lion and the adder;
   the young lion and the serpent you will trample underfoot.
"Because he holds fast to me in love, I will deliver him;
   I will protect him, because he knows my name.
When he calls to me, I will answer him;
   I will be with him in trouble;
   I will rescue him and honor him." (Ps. 91:11–15)

Reflect

Have you ever experienced the protection of a parent or older sibling? How did that help you, and how does it encourage you to know that God is protecting you right now?

Let's Pray

Father, thank You for Your strong protection and vigilant care over my life. I praise You, Lord, that Your eye of protection and care is on me for my good and for Your glory. Please direct my heart to Your steadfast love. In Jesus' name, amen.

50 *The Path to Perfect Peace*

ISAIAH 26:3-4

*"You keep him in perfect peace
whose mind is stayed on you,
because he trusts in you.
Trust in the LORD forever,
for the LORD GOD is an everlasting rock."*

There is a strong connection between the mind and the heart. The mind's contemplations reveal the heart's affections. The one whose mind is "stayed on" the Lord is the one whose heart's trust is in the Lord. That is to say that for me to trust in God is for me to keep my mind fixed on God. We see a similar correlation in Colossians where Paul writes,

> Since, then, you have been raised with Christ, set your hearts on things above, where Christ is, seated at the right hand of God. Set your minds on things above, not on earthly things. For you died, and your life is now hidden with Christ in God. When Christ, who is your life, appears, then you also will appear with him in glory. (Col. 3:1–4 NIV)

The mind and the heart are inseparable. Could you say, perhaps, that the mind is the doorway to the heart? What we believe in our minds determines how we live from our hearts.

So what a promise we have here in Isaiah! "You keep him in perfect peace whose mind is stayed on you, because he trusts in you." To have our minds stayed on God is an expression, a sign, an indication that our hearts are trusting in the Lord. We can grow in trusting in God by filling our minds with His truth—truths about His sovereignty, His goodness, His holiness, His wisdom, His power, His immutability, His omniscience, His omnipresence, His great love for us in Christ—and by keeping our minds stayed, fixed, settled on these truths.

Then, our hearts will trust in Him, and we will experience the promise of this verse: perfect peace.

Reflect

How can you purpose to keep your mind fixed on the Lord throughout the hustle and bustle of your everyday life?

Let's Pray

Lord, You deserve all my mind's attention, and You're worthy of all my heart's trust. You know how prone to wander I am. Please help me keep my mind fixed on You so my heart continually trusts in You. Fill me with perfect peace in Your presence continually. Please grant me wisdom, mercy, and strength, and please incline my heart toward You and unite my heart to fear Your name. I love You, and I trust in You. In Jesus' name, amen.

51   *Divine Delays*

EXODUS 23:29-30

"I will not drive them out from before you in one year, lest the land become desolate and the wild beasts multiply against you. Little by little I will drive them out from before you, until you have increased and possess the land."

This is remarkable. In tender mercy, the Lord shares with the Israelites that their possession of the land of Canaan will be gradual and not immediate, because if it were to happen all in one year, it would be overwhelming for them. What would happen? Wild beasts would multiply and the land would become deserted and desolate. The Israelites would not be able to properly care for the property and they would not be able to defend themselves against the wildlife there.

Take note of this, dear believer. God always has a purpose in the postponements of His promises. There are benevolent reasons behind divine delays. God promised the land of Canaan to Abraham, Isaac, and Jacob and their descendants, but the realization of that promise would be gradual *for their good.*

If you haven't received a promised blessing, perhaps you are not fully ready for it—to care for and defend the blessing. Could it be that your current delays are not denials, but all a part of God's training process? Don't lose heart. Continue to believe God for His blessings to come whether presently or eventually and be willing to receive them "little by little" as wisdom allows. Immediate gratification often brings disastrous consequences. As you wouldn't hand a child the keys to a car without a process of preparation, so the Lord does not give us certain blessings until we are fully ready to receive them. Teaching, testing, and training come first as God prepares us to praise Him with the prosperity He is pining to provide.

His pauses are for your profit. Be faithful with the little and He will make you ruler over much (Luke 16:10). Remember the words of the psalmist: "For the LORD God is a sun and shield; the LORD bestows favor and honor. No good thing does he withhold from those who walk uprightly. O LORD of hosts, blessed is the one who trusts in you!" (Ps. 84:11–12).

Reflect

Are you currently experiencing any divine delays? What do those look like, and how is God speaking comfort and encouragement to you through this meditation?

Let's Pray

Father, You are wise in all Your dealings with me and all the delays that come my way. Please open my eyes that I would have wisdom from above and that I would understand the times and the seasons and know how to respond. I humble myself and submit to Your timetable. Please grant me grace to honor You as I persevere in obedience and faith. In Jesus' name, amen.

52 *Faultless*

PROVERBS 10:28

The hope of the righteous brings joy.

O ur text today speaks of the hope of the righteous. Now, apart from Jesus, the Scriptures tell us that "there is no one righteous, not even one" (Rom. 3:10 NIV). How, then, can this offer of joy apply to us? Here's how: the perfect righteousness *of Jesus* has been credited to every believer *in Jesus*.

This is the joy of the gospel—the good news that, though we could never be declared righteous in the sight of God by our own works, God in mercy provided perfect righteousness for us through His Son Jesus Christ, our Savior. Jesus never once sinned; instead He perfectly fulfilled the law of God on our behalf. When Jesus died on the cross, He received the punishment that we deserved for our sins, and in exchange provided us with His perfection. Everyone who trusts in Christ is justified by His grace as a gift and is clothed in His righteousness. When God sees a believer, He sees the righteousness of His Son (see Rom. 3:20–24).

This is tender mercy and amazing grace! "Christ Jesus . . . became to us wisdom from God, *righteousness* and sanctification and redemption" (1 Cor. 1:30). Jesus' perfect obedience to the law of God is now *ours*. Jesus' sinless life has been ascribed to us, counted as if it were our very own. Jesus' anger-free life, His guilt-free life, His lust-free life, His greed-free life, His flawless perfection of perfect love and blamelessness has been attributed to us who believe and trust in Jesus as if we had never once sinned and as if we had always perfectly obeyed the law of God in intent and actuality! This is what it means to be justified.

So, our text says, "the hope of the righteous *brings joy*." How could it be any other way? The hope of the righteous is the hope of the full acceptance, everlasting joy, and blessings and riches that Jesus alone deserves. By our sins, we had blown it, but . . .

> when the goodness and loving kindness of God our Savior
> appeared, he saved us, not because of works done by us in righteousness, but according to his own mercy, by the washing of
> regeneration and renewal of the Holy Spirit, whom he poured
> out on us richly through Jesus Christ our Savior, so that being
> justified by his grace we might become heirs according to the
> hope of eternal life. (Titus 3:4–7)

Everlasting joy is ours in Jesus for all eternity because of *His* righteousness credited to us!

Reflect

What kind of effect does it have on your soul when you
consider Jesus' perfect life credited to *you*?

Let's Pray

Jesus, thank You for living the perfect life that I could never live!
Thank You for going to the cross and bearing the punishment that
I deserve and absorbing the wrath of God in full for the sins I've
committed. Thank You for saying, "It is finished" and fulfilling
all righteousness. Thank You for rising from the grave, defeating
death and sin and Satan, so I could be fully and freely forgiven and
have the gift of eternal life through faith in Your life, death, and
resurrection. I worship You, Jesus! Amen.

53 *The Grace I Need*

PSALM 68:19

Blessed be the Lord,
who daily bears us up;
God is our salvation.

God in His wisdom keeps us dependent on Him daily, and daily He upholds us. "Blessed be the Lord who *daily* bears us up." True, someone may receive an inheritance or sell a company with a massive financial payout, but God does not give fifty years of mercy in one lump sum. Otherwise, we would fixate our joy on the gifts and not the Giver. Instead, His mercies are "new every morning," so great is His faithfulness (Lam. 3:23).

The Christian life is a life of daily dependence. Jesus teaches us to "seek first the kingdom of God and his righteousness." He adds that we needn't be anxious about the day after this one, for that will take care of itself. And anyway, "sufficient for the day is its own trouble" (Matt. 6:33–34). So the grace I need comes as I need the grace. My need is to be daily borne up, strengthened, supported, enabled, helped, upheld, empowered, and given grace from God above. That's how dependent I am, and how mercifully generous He is. With the right mindset intact, this is an exciting way to live, ever looking to the Lord for day-by-day provision.

It is both humbling and hopeful. Each night, we can rest our weary heads on a pillow of mercy, recounting all the specific ways the Lord has borne us up that day. As we look ahead to future days, let's resist the temptation to be overwhelmed with a sense of our inadequacy and remind ourselves instead that the Lord will *daily* bear us up. As the need arises, our prayers will also ascend, and the provision will appear.

Jesus reminds us to stay close. "Abide in me, and I in you. As the branch cannot bear fruit by itself, unless it abides in the vine, neither can you, unless you abide in me. I am the vine; you are the branches. Whoever abides in me and I in him, he it is that bears much fruit, for apart from me you can do nothing" (John 15:4–5).

Reflect

How have you experienced God's faithfulness and tender mercy in the way He daily bears you up? How do you need Him to bear you up right now?

Let's Pray

Lord, thank You for keeping me low in many ways and keeping me dependent on You. Thank You for the daily trials that make way for communion with You daily. Apart from You, I can do nothing. You are my salvation and my day-to-day strength and song. Every day I need You, and every day You lift me up; I look forward to the day when You will finally receive me into glory for all eternity. Even then, I will glorify You in complete dependence and joyful praise. In Jesus' name, amen.

54 *Every Gift from God*

LUKE 1:49–50

"He who is mighty has done great things for me,
and holy is his name.
And his mercy is for those who fear him
from generation to generation."

E very gift *from* God is designed to deepen our awareness of the
goodness *of* God and arouse our affections in praise *to* God. We
are to draw the line from gift to the Giver. Let us learn from Mary's
song above to string God's mercies into melodies of praise. May every
expression of His goodness remind us of His holiness and His might
and result in worship and adoration. "For he who is mighty has done
great things for me, and holy is his name." Mary's song of praise reflects
a heart of gratitude and reverential awe. Can you and I not sing a song of
praise from a similar heart of gratefulness? Hasn't the Lord done great
things for you as well?

It is true that Mary experienced unusual favor. When the angel Gabriel
announced the unexpected news that she was to be granted the privilege
of being the earthly mother of the long-expected Messiah, he called her
the "favored one" and assured the young woman that "the Lord is with
you!" (Luke 1:28). Her song of adoration is appropriate. But the baby
born to Mary in Bethlehem was born for *you*, as well. You, too, are favored
by God above. You'll remember that the angel addressing the shepherds
in Luke 2 called Jesus' birth good news "for all the people."

In her song, Mary magnifies both the character of God and the
blessings of God. Mary knows that it is the might of God's character
that has empowered the mercy of God's heart to lead to the salvation
of God's people. If God were not all-powerful, He could not do great

118

things, but God *is* almighty, as the angel Gabriel declares, "Nothing will be impossible with God" (Luke 1:37). Not only is He mighty, but He is completely set apart. No one else is like the Lord, for holy is His name, as Mary states. Further, the Lord is incomparable: "To whom then will you compare me, that I should be like him?" God asks (Isa. 40:25).

Let's learn, with Mary, to praise God for every good gift from above, starting with praise for Jesus, the greatest gift we have ever received!

Reflect

How can Mary's song of praise serve as a model for the way you commune with God?

Let's Pray

Father, I thank You that You are mighty, and You have done great things for me! Holy is Your Name. I praise You and thank You for every good and perfect gift You have given, most of all the gift of Your Son, Jesus. Thank You for providing a Savior for me and for all who trust in You. In Jesus' name, amen.

55   *What Jesus Is Preparing for Us*

"Let not your hearts be troubled. Believe in God; believe also in me. In my Father's house are many rooms. If it were not so, would I have told you that I go to prepare a place for you? And if I go and prepare a place for you, I will come again and will take you to myself, that where I am you may be also."

Several years ago, our family went through a challenging situation. Our refrigerator had leaked, causing the floors of the kitchen and dining room to buckle. Thankfully, insurance covered the cost of a hotel suite for our family while the damage was attended to in our home, and new floors were installed.

I remember feeling so displaced and concerned about all this at the time. Here I was, anxious, worried, and tempted to complain about a minor speed bump in an otherwise comfortable housing condition, when I came upon this statement from Jesus in my regular reading of the gospels: "Foxes have holes, and birds of the air have nests, but the Son of Man has nowhere to lay his head." This verse comes within a series of encounters with would-be disciples who had all sorts of reasons why they needed to delay following Him (Luke 9:57–62). Jesus pointed out that often one must leave a comfortable life to give their life to Him.

Jesus left much in heaven to come to earth, being obedient to the point of death and to prepare a place for us in paradise (Phil. 2:5–11). Can you believe it? The King of kings, the Lord of lords, the Savior, forsook His home in heaven so He could prepare an eternal home for us.

Our family spent half a month in a hotel while contractors repaired the damage due to a broken refrigerator, and that was a trial for us, but the Son of Man spent His earthly ministry with no permanent place to "lay His head" so we could rest for all eternity. Isn't that amazing grace and mercy?

Reflect

Have you ever felt displaced from your home? What was that like? How does it encourage you to hear Jesus say that He is preparing a place for you in heaven?

Let's Pray

Lord Jesus, thank You for forsaking a comfortable home during Your ministry on this earth so that You could go provide a home for us for all eternity. I believe You've gone ahead to prepare a place for me and that You are coming again to take me to Yourself, and I can't wait to see the place You have prepared! Please calm my troubled heart in Your presence and in Your promises, for Your glory, I pray. Amen.

56 *What Jesus Wants*

ISAIAH 42:3

. . . a bruised reed he will not break,
and a faintly burning wick he will not quench.

Our Savior is so full of compassion and mercy; He gently leads and sympathetically cares for the harassed and helpless and all those who have been laid low, whether through their own mistakes or the evil of others (Matt. 9:36). He does not despise the hurting or discard the cracked and shattered; rather, He is the gentlest with the most troubled of souls. If you feel bruised and damaged, Jesus wants you.

And here is your promise: "A bruised reed he will not break, and a faintly burning wick he will not quench." Perhaps you can recall former days when the flames of your love for God burned bright. When you think of that time in your life, you sigh and moan for the grace of your former years. Now, instead of focusing on thriving as you previously did, you are merely trying to survive and put one foot in front of the other, day by day, moment by moment. If that is you, you are a faintly burning wick. As such, *you can claim this promise.*

The Lord will not quench your fire. He will not douse your flame. He will not break you. He will not dispose of you or what little faith you have. No, instead, your merciful Savior will gather you in His arms and gently lead you and your faith (Isa. 40:11). He will fan it into flame until once again you are burning brightly in His honor.

Jesus was bruised for our iniquities, so He knows how to handle the bruised reed. He was wounded for our transgressions, so He knows how to handle the weak and wounded. The Lord has laid on Him the iniquity of us all (Isa. 53:5–6).

God yearns to show His mercy. He says, "If he cries to me, I will hear, *for I am compassionate*" (Ex. 22:27). The Lord is your covering in the night. He is the blanket for warming your cold heart and soul. Draw near to Him and let the flame of His love burn the faint ember of your heart until it rises as a full flame again, or for the very first time.

Reflect

Do you think of God as being compassionate, or do you think of Him in some other way? How does this meditation change your view of God and His mercy?

Let's Pray

Lord, I'm a bruised reed. Please be gentle with me, according to Your Word. I'm a faintly burning wick. Please don't quench my flame. O God, I pray that You would renew me, restore me, fan my faith into flame, and fill me with Your Holy Spirit so all would know that You are my God and that You have rescued me. In Jesus' mighty name, I pray. Amen.

57 A Mark of Spiritual Vitality

PSALM 55:22

Cast your burden on the LORD,
and he will sustain you.

D o you suppose it is a sign of strength for you to carry all your burdens alone? It is no mark of spiritual strength to even attempt to do so! But we all try, don't we?

It may be a demonstration of *physical* strength for someone to be able to lift and carry heavy weights, but a mark of the *spiritually* vivacious is the aptitude for off-loading their burdens properly.

As a fisherman is skilled in the art of casting a fly, so a believer must become proficient in the ability to correctly cast his or her cares. There are loads too heavy to be loaned to man alone; only God can bear them.

God often assigns those He loves challenges for which no human counselor will suffice. We need comfort from above and counsel from our Chief Counselor, the Holy Spirit. We fall short when we look merely horizontally for the help that can come only from God.

The text says to "cast" your burden on Him. Throw it off of yourself and let Him bear it. If we will but tell God everything about every daily thing that is distressing us, and if we will but bring to Him all our difficulties, He will uphold us with His sustaining grace. There is no burden God is unwilling to hear or unable to bear.

What are you carrying right now that is not yours to carry alone?

Every affliction is an invitation for communion with the living God. We will view our burdens as blessings when they are perceived with this divine intent. So, my soul, cast, cast, cast your burdens now on Him! Tell the Lord all your troubles. Ask Him for mercy from above, and you will experience His all-sustaining love!

"Cast your burden on the LORD, *and he will sustain you.*"

Reflect

What are you carrying that is not yours to carry alone? Why not cast your cares on the Lord right now?

Let's Pray

Father, I thank You that You are my Lord and that You have invited me to cast every burden on You. Thank You that You haven't designed me to carry everything alone. What a miserable life that would be! Lord, here's what's weighing me down right now [tell Him everything]. *Please take it off my shoulders and sustain me, for Your glory. In Jesus' name, amen.*

58   *God Never Wastes Your Pain*

PSALM 34:18

The LORD is near to the brokenhearted and saves the crushed in spirit.

Anyone who has traveled away from city lights to remote locations can attest that stars in the sky shine brightest in the darkest of nights. Though always present in the evening sky, the brilliance of their ever-glowing light is most visible to us in blackness. The bleaker the night, the more beauty we see of luminaries in the heavens.

The Christian's life is much the same. Darkness makes way for the light of Christ. God's riches are uncovered as we become aware of our need. Grace is realized amid our own depravity: "Where sin increased, grace abounded all the more" (Rom. 5:20). This is what Jesus means when He says, "Blessed are those who mourn, for they shall be comforted" (Matt. 5:4). Elsewhere He says, "Unless a kernel of wheat falls to the ground and dies, it remains only a single seed. But if it dies, it produces many seeds" (John 12:24 NIV). Losses lead to gain, joy is unearthed in sorrow, and life is rediscovered in the face of death.

Truly, the Lord comes close to the brokenhearted and saves those who are crushed in spirit. Problems open the door for God's power to be revealed; the darker things get, the more beautiful the mercy of God will shine in contrast. If you have descended into darkness, either from your own offenses or the evil around you, look up into the night sky. Your gracious God is your great Redeemer. He redeems your life from the pit (Ps. 103:4). He will bring light out of the darkness engulfing you and life out of the death all around you.

There is a paradox to life, that those who mourn the most are also those who are most fit to be comforted; those who feel their brokenness most are most apt to sense the restoration of the Healer; those who are crushed in spirit and most dashed to pieces are those who are most grateful for a Savior. The Redeemer never wastes trials, difficulties, and pain. If you are in the darkness, He is near. Look up and let the light of Christ Himself shine upon you.

Reflect

Can you remember a place where you saw the most stars in the night sky? Where were you? When have you sensed God's nearness the most? How does this comfort you in your sorrows?

Let's Pray

Father, thank You that You draw near to the brokenhearted and save the crushed in spirit. Thank You that the darker my sky gets, the more clearly I can see the glory of Your light shining through. Thank You that You summon me to take all my pain and all my heartache directly to You and You don't cast me away, You draw me close. Lord, please draw me near right now. In Jesus' name, amen.

59   *You Cannot Out-Give God*

2 CHRONICLES 25:9

Amaziah said to the man of God, "But what shall we do about the hundred talents that I have given to the army of Israel?" The man of God answered, "The LORD is able to give you much more than this."

K ing Amaziah had hired 100,000 mighty men of valor from Israel to serve as mercenaries, paying them a hundred talents of silver in advance when a prophet of the Lord appeared and instructed him to disband the mercenaries before battle.

Naturally, Amaziah was concerned that if he followed the prophet's counsel, he could end up losing the battle *and* the one hundred talents he was called to sacrifice, as well. So the prophet assures him, "The LORD is able to give you much more than this." Fortunately, he listens (this time), discharges the mercenaries, and leads his people to victory.

Whenever we're called to sacrifice for the gospel or kingdom, let this truth settle in our souls: The Lord is able to give you much more than you had asked for or expected. Our Lord continually assures us that in any and every sacrifice, He is able to repay us *exponentially*.

When Peter said to Jesus, "We have left everything and followed you," Jesus replied, "Truly, I say to you, there is no one who has left house or brothers or sisters or mother or father or children or lands, for my sake and for the gospel, who will not receive a hundredfold now in this time, houses and brothers and sisters and mothers and children and lands, with persecutions, and in the age to come eternal life" (Mark 10:28–30).

Reader, do you truly think you can out-give God? Everything is *His*. The silver is His, the gold is His, and the cattle on a thousand hills (Hag. 2:8; Ps. 50:10). The Lord rewards obedience and losses *due to acts of obedience*. If you are ousted from your home for your faith, you can expect that the Lord will open the doors for you to be welcomed in a household of faith. Blessings will always follow the faithful—if not in this life, certainly in the life to come.

Reflect

Where have you been summoned to sacrifice for the sake of the Lord and His kingdom? How does this meditation encourage you to trust God amid that sacrifice?

Let's Pray

Father, thank You that You are able to give much more than I could ever sacrifice. You've already given Your Son, Your only Son, as the greatest sacrifice this world has ever seen. No one can out-give You, Lord. I can't out-give You. Help me trust You, live for You, sacrifice for You, and walk in obedience to what You call me to do. All I have is Yours, and my life is Yours. Take my life, Lord, and let it be consecrated wholly to You. In Jesus' name, amen.

60 *Crying Out with Cracked Lips*

ISAIAH 41:17–18

When the poor and needy seek water,
and there is none,
and their tongue is parched with thirst,
I the LORD will answer them;
I the God of Israel will not forsake them.
I will open rivers on the bare heights,
and fountains in the midst of the valleys.
I will make the wilderness a pool of water,
and the dry land springs of water.

Perhaps you're in a place where you feel dry in your soul, completely parched. Maybe you're struggling with the sense that you're in a valley . . . or even a pit. The Lord knows. The Lord sees. The Lord cares for you.

This passage gently confirms your condition, your environment, your longings, and your hope. Dear reader, you are "poor and needy"—that's *your condition*. You don't have to fake it any longer; you don't have to pretend you're doing better than you are. You can freely admit your desperate need of the One who can supply all grace. The Lord will hear and answer you.

Your environment is under His control. Yes, right now it is as if you were "on the bare heights"; you can't see any evidence of fruit or life around you. You are in the valley, a place of extremes, a harsh and arid environment. You feel low because you've been brought low. I know what that's like. I, too, have been there.

You're in the dry land where the earth cracks beneath your feet. You're wandering in uncharted territory, a wilderness of undisturbed and uncontrolled ecosystems, where the wild animals roam. You're pleading for relief, for the return of plenty, for refreshment, for joy. Here, you long for water and your tongue is parched with thirst.

Dear parched one, this is your hope: when all human deliverances fail, the Lord of all creation will come through for you. The same God who made the wilderness can "make the wilderness a pool of water." The same God who created the bare heights "will open rivers on the bare heights"; the same God who made the dry land will make "the dry land springs of water"; the same God who led you into the valley will open fountains for you amid the valleys. Cry out to Him with your cracked lips and your stuttering voice and know and consider and understand that it is the hand of the Lord who delivers (Isa. 41:20). He will surely deliver *you*.

Reflect

Have you ever been in the valley spiritually? Are you there right now? How does it encourage you to know that God opens rivers on the barren heights and makes the dry land springs of water?

Let's Pray

Father, I thank You that You are in complete control of my present environment and that You are the God of great reversals. In an instant, You can turn cracked and dry land into springs of water. Please do that for me, Lord. All my springs are in You. Please open the floodgates of heaven and let the rain fall on my dry and barren heart for Your glory. In Jesus' name, amen.

61 *The Paradox of the Believer's Life*

2 CORINTHIANS 6:10

As sorrowful, yet always rejoicing.

These five words are in the Bible together to protect our sanity. God is showing us the perplexing paradox of the believer's life— that we can be simultaneously full of sorrow and yet also filled with joy. If that's you, you're not crazy. You're not strange or weird. You're a follower of the Lord living in a fallen world, looking forward to the hope of heaven.

It's the tender mercy of God to show us that sorrow and joy can not only coexist but that it's natural for them to coexist in the heart of a believer.

In a fallen world where sin abounds, how can we not be sorrowful? Every instance or indication of evil should break our hearts. And yet, we know that where sin abounds, grace abounds all the more (Rom. 5:20). We rejoice in the hope of the glory of God (Rom. 5:2). We also rejoice in our sufferings, because we know the fruit that suffering produces: endurance, character, and hope (Rom. 5:3–4).

I vividly remember the day when my father was rushed to the hospital with kidney failure and I heard the news of my uncle's death; it was the same day I baptized two of my children. I was filled with sorrow for my dad and the loss of my uncle and yet full of joy at the celebration of my children's public profession of faith in Christ. Though all these moments were extreme and simultaneous occasions, every day is filled with varying degrees of sorrow and carries with it levels of joy. Even in circumstances of heightened pleasure, Jesus instructs us: "Nevertheless, do not rejoice in this, that the spirits are subject to you, but rejoice that your names are written in heaven" (Luke 10:20).

The Lord invites us to come as we are and bring all our sorrows and all our joys to Him while we look forward to an eternity where there will be no vestiges of the fallen world. The day is coming when "He will wipe away every tear from their eyes, and death shall be no more, neither shall there be mourning, nor crying, nor pain anymore, for the former things have passed away" (Rev. 21:4).

Reflect

Have you ever been simultaneously full of sorrow and yet filled with joy? What was that like for you?

Let's Pray

Father, thank You that the day is coming when there will be no more sorrow for those in Christ. Thank You for the hope of heaven where You will wipe away every tear from our eyes and there will be no more death, no more mourning, no more crying, and no more pain. Until then, help me rejoice in You, even while I'm full of sorrow in this world, so that I can say that I'm sorrowful, yet always rejoicing. In Jesus' name, amen.

62 Invited to Receive

HEBREWS 4:16

*Let us then with confidence draw near to the throne of grace,
that we may receive mercy and find grace to help in time of need.*

God loves to hear your voice. There is absolutely nothing that you can't take to Him or share with Him. He's not irritated. He welcomes your sharing your heart, your burdens, your cares, your griefs, your sorrows, your desires; all of it you can take to the throne of grace and God welcomes it. He loves it. John Newton, who wrote "Amazing Grace," also wrote a hymn that contains these words: "Thou art coming to a King; large petitions with thee bring, for His grace and power are such, none can ever ask too much." God's grace is His unmerited, ill-deserved favor to those in Christ, and His power is that He is able to do anything you ask for in His Name.

If you are a believer and you have been given the gift of eternal life, anything you ask for in this world is *less* than what God has already given you. After all, "He who did not spare his own Son but gave him up for us all, how will he not also with him graciously give us all things?" (Rom. 8:32).

You can absolutely pour out your entire heart before God, and He will receive you. If you are not experiencing immediate answers to prayer, understand that God's delays are not necessarily His denials. If a desire persists, continue to ask God for it and wait and watch and see what He does. His deferments teach us to pray. If God gave us everything right when we asked for it, we would take the gifts and cease our prayers and that would not be good for our souls.

So thank God for His delays that keep you praying and drawing near to Him. At the very least what you are going to get is sweet communion with God Almighty. He may also give you your heart's desire and grant you what you are asking for; so ask away; go to God with all your requests, and experience the grace that only He can give.

No eye has seen, nor ear heard,
    nor the heart of man imagined,
what God has prepared for those who love him—(1 Cor. 2:9)

Reflect

Do you live and pray as if you believe that God loves to hear your voice?

Let's Pray

Father, thank You for sitting on a throne of grace and inviting me to come to You to receive mercy and find grace in my time of need. I'm amazed by how generous and gracious and merciful You are. So, I draw near to You right now in confidence that I'll be met with mercy. Hear my prayers, Lord, and be glorified in meeting my needs as I share them all with You. In Jesus' name I pray. Amen.

63 *Wisdom from Above*

JAMES 3:17-18

But the wisdom from above is first pure, then peaceable, gentle, open to reason, full of mercy and good fruits, impartial and sincere. And a harvest of righteousness is sown in peace by those who make peace.

What if bravery in this world looked like kindness? What if the most courageous thing that you or I could do is to love other people? What if strength was most clearly displayed as empathy, compassion, care, loving concern, and a desire for the good of others? What kind of power would this display in an angry world full of rage?

Power from above. Grace from above. *Wisdom from above.*

Christ became for us the wisdom of God (1 Cor. 1:30). Jesus offers weary sinners *rest.* He did not come into the world to condemn the world, but in order that the world would be saved through Him (John 3:17). Out of the overflow of His gentleness comes rest and peace for our souls. Isn't it amazing to consider that Jesus consistently set broken people at ease? He was full of mercy toward the undeserving.

Recall Jesus' description of Himself in Matthew 11:28–30. He used words like "gentle" and "lowly in heart," and He offered rest and a light burden. Jesus is not pugnacious. He isn't looking for a fight. He isn't on a search for our faults. Instead, He's on a mission of mercy. That's the wisdom from above.

May we, too, be people who set others at ease with tenderness, remembering that it is only because of the mercy of the Lord that we even know the Lord.

Have you ever thought of courage and strength being displayed through empathy and compassion? Why does it take bravery to show kindness to others?

Let's Pray

Father, thank You for Your wisdom. Thank You for sending Jesus to become for us the wisdom of God. Lord, I need wisdom from above, and I'm so grateful that You have said, "If any of you lack wisdom, let him cry out to the One who gives freely to all without finding fault, and it will be given." Lord, I cry out to You right now for wisdom from above—wisdom that is pure, peaceable, gentle, open to reason, full of mercy and good fruits, impartial and sincere. Please give me this wisdom and let it display the certainty that the God of Wisdom is with me. In Jesus' name I pray. Amen.

64 Remembering Jesus

2 TIMOTHY 2:8

Remember Jesus Christ.

It is so easy for us to focus on what we have or haven't done for God that we forget *what God has done for us.* Yet our ultimate joy is never in what we're doing for God. It's in what God has done *for us.* That's why I have this verse hanging on the wall of my home office:

2 TIMOTHY 2:8

REMEMBER JESUS CHRIST

What an incredible exhortation! I find it so fascinating that at the end of his life, the apostle Paul's most practical advice to his son in the faith, Timothy, was to "remember Jesus Christ." You would think that this is so elementary that no mature believer should ever need to hear it, but that is simply not the case. We *all* need this daily reminder precisely because we so easily forget.

Forgetfulness is our neutral gear. After three decades of following Christ, I have come to realize that I have never outgrown—and will never outgrow—the need for this simple and yet profound life-giving reminder to remember Jesus Christ.

I could forget everything else I have ever known, everyone in my life could abandon me, and I could lose every possession that I have, but if I remember Jesus Christ, then I remember everything I need to know. Jesus is the author and perfecter of my faith, the one who sustains me and provides me with life, breath, and everything I need.

This is key to basking in the goodness and grace and mercy and love of God: Remember Jesus Christ. If you are wondering if God loves you, *He does*: remember Jesus Christ. "For God so loved the world, that he gave his only Son, that whoever believes in him should not perish but have eternal life" (John 3:16). Jesus remembers us: "I am the good shepherd. I know my own and my own know me, just as the Father knows me and I know the Father; and I lay down my life for the sheep" (John 10:14–15).

If you are wondering if your life matters, *it does*: remember Jesus Christ. "Greater love has no one than this, that someone lay down his life for his friends" (John 15:13). He loves you. Your life matters. As we get our eyes off ourselves and set our eyes on Jesus, we will be filled with joy and be able to serve others in that joy and make an impact on the world around us.

"If then you have been raised with Christ, seek the things that are above, where Christ is, seated at the right hand of God. Set your minds on things that are above, not on things that are on earth." This is remembering Jesus. Why? "For you have died, and your life is hidden with Christ in God. When Christ who is your life appears, then you also will appear with him in glory" (Col. 3:1–4).

Reflect

Are there particular ways you are most prone to forget Jesus? What does it look like for you when you forget Jesus, and how can you intentionally seek to remember Him daily?

Let's Pray

Father, thank You so much that You loved me enough to give Your Son to secure my salvation. I'm so grateful for Your love. Lord Jesus, thank You that You loved me so much that You willingly laid down Your life for me, even to the point of death on a cross. Holy Spirit, thank You for loving me and opening the eyes of my heart to understand these truths. God, please help me always remember Jesus Christ, the focal point and proof of Your love for me. It's in Jesus' name I pray. Amen.

65 *Comfort in a Culture of Criticism*

1 CORINTHIANS 4:1-5

This is how one should regard us, as servants of Christ and stewards of the mysteries of God. Moreover, it is required of stewards that they be found faithful. But with me it is a very small thing that I should be judged by you or by any human court. In fact, I do not even judge myself. For I am not aware of anything against myself, but I am not thereby acquitted. It is the Lord who judges me. Therefore do not pronounce judgment before the time, before the Lord comes, who will bring to light the things now hidden in darkness and will disclose the purposes of the heart. Then each one will receive his commendation from God.

What a freeing and comforting text for all of us who struggle with the approval of others! This text reminds me that in Christ I have been set free from the bondage of living for the fluctuating approval of others or the fleeting glory of my own accomplishments; Christ is my righteousness, and all the approval I'll ever need is found in Him.

Everyone in my life is put there by God for a purpose. The Lord has put others in my life, and me in others' lives, to effect His purpose. I should see myself as a servant of Christ and a steward of the mysteries of God, and this is how others should regard me, as well. My focus should be faithfulness to God's call, not the opinions of others. To his readers, the apostle Paul is essentially saying, "It matters very little what you think of me, what any human court thinks of me, or even what I think of myself; what matters is what the Lord thinks of me."

We live in a culture cradled by criticism, giving full vent to viral fury; it's a society of rage. Wisely does the writer of Ecclesiastes instruct us, "Do not take to heart all the things that people say, lest you hear your servant cursing you. Your heart knows that many times you yourself have cursed others" (Eccl. 7:21–22). Oh, that we would all heed the counsel of our text and place a hand over our critical mouths: *"Therefore do not pronounce judgment before the time, before the Lord comes."* How would observing this admonition affect the cultural landscape, our thoughts, our words, and our engagement with social media? Ephesians says, "Let no corrupting talk come out of your mouths, but only such as is good for building up, as fits the occasion, that it may give grace to those who hear" (Eph. 4:29).

Here's what's incredible: when the Lord comes, He will bring to light the things now hidden in darkness and will disclose the purposes of the heart and "then each one will receive his commendation from God." The Lord is leaning forward *ready to commend, not to condemn*! Can you see that here? Amazing grace. Unfathomable mercy. Oh, that we would do the same! Suspend every other judgment and wait until the Lord comes to commend any good that He has wrought in you! God is looking for grace in you!

Reflect

In what ways do you struggle with living for the fluctuating approval of others or the fleeting glory of your own accomplishments? How does this meditation console you in those areas?

Let's Pray

Father, I praise You that in Christ I have been set free from the bondage of living for the fluctuating approval of others and the fleeting glory of my own accomplishments. Jesus is my righteousness, and all the approval I'll ever need is found in Him. Father, please enable me increasingly to view myself and others with Your perspective, and thank You for leaning forward ready to commend and not condemn me! Holy Spirit, please give me the heart of Christ for others. In Jesus' name I pray. Amen.

66 *God Is Not Like Us*

DEUTERONOMY 4:31

For the LORD your God is a merciful God. He will not leave you or destroy you or forget the covenant with your fathers that he swore to them.

People are ruthless: People leave, people destroy, and people forget and forsake their promises. It's been said "the best of men are men at best" and this is true. God is not like us. The Lord is merciful: the Lord stays, the Lord builds up, and the Lord remembers and is faithful to all His promises. Because He is not like us, we can trust Him and entrust ourselves to Him.

God has promised to never leave us or forsake us (Heb. 13:5b) and He is faithful to His promises (Josh. 21:45; Ps. 145:13b). People may have failed and forsaken you, but God never will. The Lord has committed that He will be with us until the end of the age and He has promised that He will preserve and sustain us to the very end (see 1 Cor. 1:8–9). God remembers His covenant and guarantees to never violate His covenant (Ps. 89:34). Because God does not lie, and because the covenant He makes with His people is an everlasting covenant, you can trust Him and entrust yourself fully to Him. He will prove to be faithful to you, and you will rejoice in His steadfast love and mercy to the very end!

> The LORD is gracious and merciful.
> He provides food for those who fear him;
>   he remembers his covenant forever.
> He has shown his people the power of his works,
>   in giving them the inheritance of the nations.

The works of his hands are faithful and just;
all his precepts are trustworthy. (Ps. 111:4–7)

Reflect

Have you ever been left, forgotten, or forsaken by others? If so, has this tainted your view of God in any way? How does this meditation help you see the difference between that experience and God's faithfulness to you?

Let's Pray

O Great God of Abraham, Isaac, and Jacob, thank You for Your faithfulness and steadfast love. You are a merciful and gracious God, and You will not forget the covenant You have made. You are trustworthy, and I put all my trust in You and in Your promises. Please fill me with Your Spirit and exalt the Son of David and the Son of God, Jesus Christ, in and through me for Your glory. In Jesus' name I pray. Amen.

67 *From God's Perspective*

COLOSSIANS 3:11

Here there is not Greek and Jew, circumcised and uncircumcised,
barbarian, Scythian, slave, free; but Christ is all, and in all.

E*very one* of us matters so much to God. You may feel insignificant.
You may feel of little value. But *your* life is certainly significant, and
God has a place for you at His table of grace.

There is no spiritual inequality for believers in Christ. None *at all.*
There are no status distinctions based on ethnicity, culture, social influence, financial position, age, or any other factor. No one has less dignity
than any other. Everyone stands on the same level at the foot of the
cross and faith in Christ removes all separations. Jesus breaks down every barrier so that we are all one in Christ Jesus. If you are in Christ, you
are accepted in the beloved, and you have no less privilege than Paul,
who penned the verse above inspired by the Holy Spirit.

You may think, "Who am I? I have nothing to offer to God." But
God doesn't need anything from you. Salvation, from first to last, is
all of grace. You and I don't need to do or accomplish anything to be
loved or accepted by God. The gospel—*the good news that Christ died
for sinners*—tells us that God doesn't relate to you and me based on
our advantages or our merits or our performance. So, just as no one is
accepted by God based on personal advantages, so no one is rejected by
God for the lack of them, or because of any disadvantage or distinction.
All who sincerely believe on the Lord Jesus Christ become *children of
God and heirs of heaven*—no matter their nationality, background, culture, or condition.

The renowned eighteenth-century Bible commentator Matthew
Henry said, "The gospel excludes none that do not exclude themselves."[4]

In other words, He will have us if we will but open our hearts to Him and respond to the invitation.

If we want to make a difference in the world for Christ, we have to see things from God's eyes. In Jesus, all barriers are removed, and bridges are constructed. Jesus unites us in tender mercy. Now, this doesn't mean our differences no longer exist; but it does mean that those difference no longer have to create obstacles to our fellowship; instead, they can *flavor* our fellowship as brothers and sisters *in Christ, in the One who opens His arms to all who call on Him.* Believers belong to each other in a way that all differences that formerly divided can now be celebrated, and that is glorious because that's what heaven will be like where *Christ* is *all,* and in *all!*

Reflect

Have you ever felt like you had to accomplish something to be loved and accepted by God? How does this meditation transform your view of this? How can this positively affect your relationships with the different people in your life?

Let's Pray

Father, thank You that salvation, from first to last, is all of grace! Thank You that I don't need to do or accomplish anything to be loved or accepted by You. Thank You for not relating to me based on my own merits and for not rejecting me for the lack of any merits, but for relating to me on the basis of the perfect righteousness of Your Son, Jesus. Holy Spirit, please exalt Jesus in my heart and my life, for the glory of God the Father. In Jesus' name I pray. Amen.

---

4. Matthew Henry, Commentary on Luke 14, https://www.biblestudytools.com/commentaries/matthew-henry-complete/luke/14.html.

68 Still, There Is Room

LUKE 14:23

The master said to the servant, "Go out to the highways and hedges and compel people to come in, that my house may be filled."

I recently attended a conference with no assigned seats for the dinner reception and, despite being a fortysomething adult, when I walked into the room for the meal, I was thinking, "Where do I sit?" We all still have a bit of our sixth-grade-lunch-table selves in us, don't we? We can all experience the social anxiety of "Where do I fit in?" and "Who are my people?" and "Am I truly welcome here?"

I love the heart of Jesus displayed in our passage. Jesus wants *His house* filled to the brim, and through His actions, He communicates that He obliterates all cliques. Jesus' very heart is drawn to the outcasts, the forgotten, the excluded, the otherwise uninvited, and the left-out, and He says, "Friend, there's a seat at My table for you." Jesus came to invite the broken to the banquet of His grace. In the parable in Luke 14, a host had invited many to his banquet, but just as many made up excuses why they could not come. He instructed his servant to "bring in the poor and crippled and blind and lame," which the servant did. There was still room. That's when the master said to "Go out to the highways and hedges and compel people to come in, that my house may be filled."

It's remarkable that the title "friend of sinners" was initially a harsh critique hurled on Jesus by the religious elite of His time because to any who are aware of their brokenness and sin, it is the sweetest music the ears can hear. The Savior made sinners feel comfortable in His presence. They were drawn to Him like moths are drawn to a light in an evening sky. Jesus enjoyed spending time with unbelievers and made them feel relaxed and at ease in His presence. Why else do you think crowds flocked to Jesus? It was enjoyable to be with Him, *and they felt accepted.*

What impresses Jesus, what gets His attention, what brings blessing from the Lord is not a stuffy atmosphere of privileged religious elitism. It's a love for the hurting, compassion for the destitute, mercy for the weak, help for the needy, heart for the downtrodden, the welcoming-in of the lost— the intentional pursuit of the broken. It's open arms. *We invite the broken to feast at our tables, so they have a taste of what it's like to feast at His.* We invite others to join us in our mess, so we can watch what Christ alone can do in theirs. If we are to reflect the heart of God, we will tenderly open our arms wide, graciously extend the invitation, and watch the Savior do His work.

Reflect

When's the last time you felt like a sixth grader walking into a lunchroom, wondering where you fit in? Why do *you* think crowds of broken people flocked to Jesus?

Let's Pray

Lord Jesus, thank You for opening Your arms wide to the broken, the left-out, the hurting, the outcasts, and the otherwise forgotten. You are so gracious and so generous. I gladly accept Your invitation. Help me have a heart for others the way You have opened Your heart to me. Use me to extend this invitation to others, for Your glory. In Your name I pray. Amen.

69   *The Tender Mercy of Our God*

LUKE 1:77–78

*[John will] "give knowledge of salvation to his people
in the forgiveness of their sins,
because of the tender mercy of our God,
whereby the sunrise shall visit us from on high."*

Grasp the glory of the tender mercy of our God in this text! It is right here before you! This is not just Zechariah's story, but ours as well. John—we know him as John the Baptist—was born to Zechariah and Elizabeth in their advanced age, to prepare the way for our Savior and to give knowledge of salvation to God's people in the forgiveness of sins. Though Zechariah was initially skeptical that he and his wife would indeed be blessed with a child, God was relentlessly merciful.

If you, too, have struggled with unbelief, let this encourage you: *God does not treat us as our doubts deserve.* The Lord's mercy is not dependent on our righteousness; if it was, it would no longer be mercy. God is tender with the doubter, and He instructs us to do the same: "Have mercy on those who doubt" (Jude 22). There is more than enough sympathy for your suspicions, more than enough tenderness for your toughness, more than enough mercy for your unbelief. As theologian Richard Sibbes has written, "There is more mercy in Christ than sin in us."[5]

Zechariah comes to acknowledge that God has acted mightily, mercifully, and irreversibly to bring about salvation for His people, all because of His tender mercy. The gospel *is* the tender mercy of God. The sunrise from on high is a reference to the coming of Christ, sun of righteousness rising with healing in His wings (Mal. 4:2). Jesus came to give life and

---

5. Richard Sibbes, *The Bruised Reed* (1630; repr., Carlisle, PA: Banner of Truth, 2021), 13.

light. "For God, who said, 'Let light shine out of darkness,' has shone in our hearts to give the light of the knowledge of the glory of God in the face of Jesus Christ" (2 Cor. 4:6). The glory of Jesus is vitamin D for your soul. We are meant to enjoy the sun (and enjoy the Son), to lift our heads and to bask in the warmth of His glory. The best place to warm our cold hearts is by the fire of God's tender mercy.

Here's what Jesus came to bring: the forgiveness of sins, the gift of salvation, and the promise of eternal life. All of this is possible because of the tender mercy of our God. Let His mercy have a tenderizing effect on your soul. Bathe in it; bask in it; relish it. You have been visited from on high by overwhelming, overflowing tender mercy!

Reflect

Have you ever considered that God is tender with the doubter, has sympathy for the suspicious, and is merciful to the skeptical? How does that encourage you in your own doubts? How does it help you for your interactions with those who doubt?

Let's Pray

Father, thank You that You don't treat us as our doubts deserve, that You are tender with the doubter, and that You have more than enough mercy for my unbelief. I do believe. Lord, help me overcome my unbelief. Show me Your grace and Your glory, even as You have shown me Your mercy. In Jesus' name I pray. Amen.

70 *What God Gives*

John answered, "A person cannot receive even one thing unless it is given him from heaven."

Oh, how many of us boast of what we have been freely given as a gift! Our hands receive a mercy, and our hearts respond with conceit. Father, forgive us for such haughtiness and pride. John the Baptist had the proper view: with every tender mercy he received, he exalted Christ. Let us do the same.

Some may respond, "I've worked hard for everything I have." But let me ask you this, dear reader: Who gave you the strength and the ability to work so hard? Who gave you the inclination and the tenacity to persist in your labor and the accumulation of all your wealth? Is it not from the Lord that all your wealth has come? The Israelites were warned by Moses about the propensity to forget the Lord when experiencing prosperity, and we would all do well to take heed of that warning as well:

> "Take care lest you forget the LORD your God by not keeping his commandments and his rules and his statutes, which I command you today, lest, when you have eaten and are full and have built good houses and live in them, and when your herds and flocks multiply and your silver and gold is multiplied and all that you have is multiplied, then your heart be lifted up, and you forget the LORD your God." (Deut. 8:11–14)

Moses continued, reminding the people of what God had done for them in bringing them out of their slavery in Egypt. He reviewed the years in the wilderness and how the Lord provided for the people.

He warned them not to take credit for what the Lord had done for them: "Beware lest you say in your heart, 'My power and the might of my hand have gotten me this wealth'" (v. 17).

God is the One who gives us life and breath and *everything else* (Acts 17:25), including the power to get wealth. So do not be deceived, dear soul: "Every good gift and every perfect gift is from above, coming down from the Father of lights, with whom there is no variation or shadow due to change" (James 1:17). God gives the ability to speak, to hear, to see, to work hard, to get wealth. A person cannot receive even one thing unless it is given him from heaven. Every gift from above should draw our attention to the tender mercy of our God and should result in praise and glory to God. Let us count our blessings and give thanks to God for all that He has done for us.

Reflect

"What do you have that you did not receive?" (1 Cor. 4:7). "Let the one who boasts, boast in the Lord" (1 Cor. 1:31). Is there anything in your life that you're tempted to take full credit for or to boast about? What's the proper response to that temptation?

Let's Pray

Lord God, everything I have has come from You. I owe my life, my breath, and everything else to Your goodness and mercy. Please forgive me for ever claiming that the gifts that You have so graciously provided are products of my own power and might. It's all from You. Thank You for being so good to me, and please fill me with the Holy Spirit so I constantly give You all the glory. In Jesus' name, amen.

71   *Peace with God, Purpose in Life*

EPHESIANS 2:8-10

For by grace you have been saved through faith. And this is not your own doing; it is the gift of God, not a result of works, so that no one may boast. For we are his workmanship, created in Christ Jesus for good works, which God prepared beforehand, that we should walk in them.

To have both *peace with God* and *purpose in life* is a glorious mercy. Believer, that is what you have! You have been saved by grace, through faith, as a gift from above, not because of any good that you have done, but despite the wrong that you have done. You have peace with God and what a mercy this is. You have also been given purpose in life: to glorify Jesus through the good works He has given you to do. What a gift!

Your good works do not earn favor *with* God, but they do exalt the mercy *of* God. Jesus said, "Let your light shine before others, so that they may see your good works and give glory to your Father who is in heaven" (Matt. 5:16). Jesus gave Himself for us to redeem us from all lawlessness and to purify for Himself a people who are zealous for good works (Titus 2:14). So, we are to "be ready for every good work" and to learn to "devote [ourselves] to good works" to "help cases of urgent need, and not be unfruitful" (Titus 3:1, 8, 14).

The writer of Hebrews says we are to consider how we might "stir up one another to love and good works" (10:24). Paul says we are "to be rich in good works, to be generous and ready to share" (1 Tim. 6:18), and that good works are obvious but "even those that are not cannot remain hidden" for long (5:25). James says that the wise and understanding among us are to show their good works in the meekness of wisdom by their good conduct (3:13). Galatians says we're to not grow weary in doing good, for at the proper time we will reap a harvest if we do not give up (6:9).

The Lord wants to encourage our *zeal for good works*. Even a cynical and hostile world celebrates virtue: "Now who is there to harm you if you are zealous for what is good?" (1 Peter 3:13). We can possibly minimize hostility through courtesy and kindness. If we give ourselves to doing good works and serving others in love, *generally* others won't try to harm us. It's unusual for those who are zealous for good to be mistreated. People don't typically turn against those who are serving and benefitting the society around them. However, we'll talk in the next meditation for when that is the case.

May our conversation be full of grace, seasoned with salt, so we know how to answer everyone even as we are zealous for good works for the glory of God's tender mercy (Col. 4:6; Titus 3:8)!

Reflect

What good works are you zealous for right now? Are there any new good works you believe God is calling you to focus on, for His glory?

Let's Pray

Father, thank You for the gift of salvation, which is by Your grace and not a result of my own works. Thank You, also, for creating me in Christ Jesus to do good works, which You have prepared in advance that I should walk in. Holy Spirit, please strengthen me and fill me with zeal for every good work. May my life and my service bring much glory to God above! In Jesus' name, amen.

72 *Suffering for Righteousness' Sake*

1 PETER 2:19

For this is a gracious thing, when, mindful of God, one endures sorrows while suffering unjustly.

S ometimes we suffer, not because of any wrong we have done, but precisely *because we are doing good*. All throughout Scripture, we see the godly suffering for righteousness' sake.

Joseph refused the advances of Potiphar's wife, and he was falsely accused, maligned, and thrown in prison—*he suffered for righteousness' sake*. Daniel was a man of faithful prayer, and his enemies used that very habit to scheme against him: they set up a law against prayer and had Daniel thrown into a den of lions. Though he was rescued, *he was suffering for righteousness' sake*. Job was esteemed as a righteous man, and *that's the very thing that invited suffering into his life*, as Satan targeted him and requested permission from God to afflict him. David refused to lift a hand to harm God's anointed king, and yet Saul consistently pursued David to kill him. David was on the run for his very life—*suffering for righteousness' sake*.

All over the world and in the annals of history, Christians have suffered for their faith. We, too, are not immune from the insults, cold shoulders, intimidations, threats, scorn, maltreatment, and abuse that can come as a result of our faith. But here is tender mercy:

> If when you do good and suffer for it you endure, this is a gracious thing in the sight of God. For to this you have been called, because Christ also suffered for you, leaving you an example, so

that you might follow in his steps. He committed no sin, neither was deceit found in his mouth. When he was reviled, he did not revile in return; when he suffered, he did not threaten, but continued entrusting himself to him who judges justly. He himself bore our sins in his body on the tree, that we might die to sin and live to righteousness. By his wounds you have been healed. (1 Peter 2:20–24)

Doing what is right does not guarantee a trouble-free life. We may even *suffer* for doing right, but if you do, you can take heart that you are following directly in the footsteps of your glorious Savior, and it is a gracious thing in the sight of God to endure sorrows while suffering unjustly. The Lord sees everything you are walking through, and He Himself will reward you.

Reflect

Are there moments in your life when you believe you have suffered for righteousness' sake? Are there times when you have endured sorrows while suffering unjustly? What did those moments look like, and how does this meditation comfort, strengthen, and encourage you?

Let's Pray

Father, I'm so grateful that You see everything I'm walking through, including the times I've endured sorrow while suffering unjustly. Jesus, thank You for Your example of suffering for righteousness' sake. Holy Spirit, please strengthen me amid all suffering in this life so that everyone who looks at my life sees the grace and glory of God on display. I pray all of this in Jesus' name, amen.

73 The Greatest Act of Kindness We Can Give

JOHN 1:42

He brought him to Jesus.

Andrew brought his brother Peter to Jesus. What a mercy this was! Introducing someone to Jesus is *the* single greatest act of kindness you can bestow upon them. It may also be the single greatest act of service you can do for the church. If you've read the book of Acts, you know that Peter was the one who stood up and preached on the day of Pentecost where three thousand people received the word and responded with faith in Christ. That moment marked the beginning of the Christian church (Acts 2).

The impact of Peter's life on Christendom cannot be overstated, and Andrew is responsible for making that introduction. What a tender mercy to both men, and to the church. Some have suggested that this introduction from Andrew was perhaps as great a service to the church as anyone has ever done. We have no idea what Jesus is going to do *in* someone's life or *through* someone's life when we introduce them to Jesus.

I love the recollection of Charles Spurgeon's testimony. Spurgeon was a renowned nineteenth-century Baptist preacher whom God used in powerful ways (and still uses mightily through his writings). He is responsible for winning countless souls to Christ. Spurgeon recalls that God sent a snowstorm one Sunday morning while he was walking to church and, since he could go no farther, he turned in to a Primitive Methodist Chapel with about twelve people in attendance. The pastor was not able to make it as he was snowed in, and a common man took his place to minister the Word from Isaiah 45:22: "Look unto me, and be saved, all the ends of the earth."

A simple, uneducated man was used by God to ignite a flame of faith in Charles Spurgeon who later became one of the greatest preachers to ever herald the gospel of grace.

We don't have to have all the answers. Like Andrew, we simply follow Jesus, we walk with Jesus, and then in love we invite others to come and see for themselves, and then we watch what only Jesus can do!

Reflect

Do you believe that introducing someone to Jesus is the single greatest act of kindness you can bestow upon them? Why? Who have you introduced to Jesus, and who would you like to introduce to Him? (Take some time to pray for that individual now.)

Let's Pray

Father, I thank You now for the person who brought me to Jesus. You knew exactly what I needed, and You were so kind to me to use an imperfect individual to grasp my hand and take me to the sinless Savior who died for my sins. Holy Spirit, please use me to be that person for someone else. I want to share the love, grace, and mercy of Christ. In Jesus' name I pray. Amen.

74 *Blessed in Christ*

EPHESIANS 1:3

*Blessed be the God and Father of our Lord Jesus Christ, who has
blessed us in Christ with every spiritual blessing in the heavenly places.*

W e either have every spiritual blessing in the heavenly places, or
we are devoid of all of them. There is no middle ground, and
there is no hierarchy here. We either have all of Christ, or none of Him.
The gospel tells every believer that because of the death of Christ on
your behalf, you have been reconciled to God and are now at peace with
God (Rom. 5:1); you also have access by faith to the grace of God (Rom.
5:2). You are no longer at enmity with God, but the Lord is now favorably disposed to you based on your union with Christ (Rom. 8:31–32).

Not only that, but God has promised to work all things in your life
together for your good and His glory, conforming you to the image of His
Son (Rom. 8:28). So nothing on earth can separate you from the love of
God in Christ Jesus (Rom. 8:38–39). God forgives your sins, redeems
your life, crowns you with steadfast love and mercy, and satisfies you with
good (Ps. 103:1–5). He rewards you when you seek Him (Heb. 11:6)
and credits you with the righteousness of your Savior, Jesus Christ (2 Cor.
5:21). The gospel tells you that Jesus' perfect life has been credited to you
and now you are an heir to eternal life (Titus 3:7).

Who wouldn't want to draw near to such a merciful, gracious, and
loving Lord? Who wouldn't want others to experience the same? This
understanding not only affects our desire to draw near to God, but it
also affects our desire to share the love of Christ with others in our life:

> From now on, therefore, we regard no one according to the
> flesh. Even though we once regarded Christ according to the

flesh, we regard him thus no longer. Therefore, if anyone is in Christ, he is a new creation. The old has passed away; behold, the new has come. All this is from God, who through Christ reconciled us to himself and gave us the ministry of reconciliation; that is, in Christ God was reconciling the world to himself, not counting their trespasses against them, and entrusting to us the message of reconciliation. (2 Cor. 5:16–19)

Everyone will stand before God. Let's help others stand before Him *reconciled, accepted, forgiven, and blessed.*

Reflect

What spiritual blessing are you most grateful for right now? Who would you like to help experience these blessings as well?

Let's Pray

I bless You, God and Father of the Lord Jesus Christ! Thank You for blessing me in Christ with every spiritual blessing in the heavenly places. Holy Spirit, please help me understand more and more every blessing that is already mine through my union with Christ and to give You all the glory for it. I pray this in Jesus' name, amen.

75 *When You're Dazed and Confused*

PSALM 56:3

When I am afraid, I put my trust in you.

Y ears ago, I watched my nine-year-old son playing in the ocean during a family vacation. When we first got there, Joshua didn't worry at all about the waves. He just dove in headfirst and attacked the sea with full abandon. He wore a life jacket only because his parents made him.

Then, it happened . . . he got rolled by a monstrous wave. It wasn't an "over, under, or through" type of wave. It was an all-out sucker punch. He had no time to react. The wave just came over him like an uppercut, and Joshua took it directly on the chin. Driven harshly into the bank, he lost his breath, cut his lip on the sand, and tasted the salt water's sting.

Unfamiliar emotions entered my son's soul. He felt dazed and confused, not reactions he'd previously associated with the ocean. Fear. It took him two full days and a lot of encouragement before he ventured back into the water.

On one of those days confined to the shore, we talked about what David said in Psalm 56: "When I am afraid, I put my trust in you. In God, whose word I praise, in God I trust; I shall not be afraid" (vv. 3–4). These verses help me tremendously because I, too, struggle with fear. I told my son that my fear may look different from his, but the truth is that there are many times when I'm very afraid, and it helps me to know that King David struggled with fear too.

I often approach life a lot like Joshua was approaching the ocean. I dive in laughing . . . until I get smacked around. Then everything changes. Knocked over relationally, I'm less apt to dive back in. Disillusioned by hope deferred, I keep my dreams to myself. Sometimes, it's easier just to say, "I'm not doing that again." But then I think about all I'm missing and wonder if there's another way of dealing with my fear than pulling back.

I see another way in this psalm. I like how David admits his fear in this verse. And then he goes to God with it.

I encouraged Joshua to talk to the Lord, to battle his fear through prayer. I grinned when Joshua got back into the ocean, this time with a healthy respect for the waves and a greater appreciation for the God who controls them and who helps us battle our fears.

As I survey the landscape of my own life, I can relate. The truth is, I've been knocked around a few times. And every time it happens, I'm less likely to dive in to the deep end and more tempted to fear. But now, I'm beginning to see fear as an invitation to go to God in my trembling and put my trust in Him. Isn't it good to know that we can be honest with the Lord about our fears, and because of His tender mercy, He will set our hearts at ease and give us courage and peace?

Reflect

Have you ever been rolled over by the waves of this life and then struggled with the desire to get back into the ocean of certain situations? Are there any fears in your life that you have trouble admitting or acknowledging? How does this meditation comfort and encourage you?

Let's Pray

Father, thank You that I can be honest with You about all my fears and that instead of shaming me, You meet me with mercy and grace. So, here's what I'm afraid of right now [share your fears]. Lord, when I'm afraid, I put my trust in You. Help me. Strengthen me. Steady me, and deliver me from my fears, for Your glory. In Jesus' mighty name I pray. Amen.

76 *What God Is Waiting For*

ISAIAH 30:18

Therefore the LORD waits to be gracious to you,
and therefore he exalts himself to show mercy to you.
For the LORD is a God of justice;
blessed are all those who wait for him.

Leaning against the tall, black signpost at the crosswalk, my eyes move upward toward the walk sign, my feet eagerly anticipating the indication that it is safe to cross the busy intersection. An automated voice repeatedly commands me to *wait.* "Wait" . . . "Wait." Finally, I hear the welcome phrase, "The walk sign is on."

At its prompting, I amble along the street, glad but contemplative. I wonder how much of my life has been spent waiting . . . waiting for progress on lifelong prayers, dreams, hopes, and desires. Now, I'm waiting on the crosswalk sign that says it's safe to proceed.

Waiting may be a part of the small things in life, but it's a major part of our lives as a whole. So much of life is spent in waiting. It's easy to grow weary while we wait. The truth is, for the Christian, all of life is one big, steady wait. There is anticipation, a longing, and a yearning that is natural for the believer on this side of eternity. And even the creation is waiting for redemption (Rom. 8:19, 23).

In this world, we will never outgrow our waiting. Every day brings some new measure of waiting. The pain of it is with us at the dawn of every new morning even as the dew kisses the grass and the birds greet the light with melodies. Yet God's mercies are also new every morning, which makes the waiting worthwhile. God upholds us with sustaining grace when He calls us to stand in line and wait.

It's helpful to know that waiting is a major part of God's plan for us.

If you're waiting on God, you are not alone. The Lord enrolls each of His children in this university. Abraham waited for a son, Joseph waited for justice, Moses waited for a peek at the promised land, David waited to become king.

Even if you have your desires delivered, ultimately God has placed eternity into our hearts, and we are in a constant craving for the future day when His glory will be fully revealed in us and through us. One day, the complete realization of our inheritance in Christ will finally be ours. Then we will be fully redeemed and there will be no more waiting. For now, we live with the reality that our best life is *then*, not now. If you're growing weary in your waiting, remember that you're not alone. The Lord works on behalf of those who wait for Him (Isa. 64:4). And He, also, is waiting . . . to be gracious *to you* (Isa. 30:18).

What a merciful, gracious, and kind God we have, waiting to show us grace and mercy.

Reflect

Is there anything you've waited on for a long time before it became a reality? Is there anything you're waiting on right now? How does it encourage you to know that the Lord waits to be gracious to you, and He exalts Himself to show mercy to you?

Let's Pray

Lord, waiting is hard. I admit that I don't often like to wait, that I want things to happen quickly, and that I'm so often in a rush to see the benefit of all my labors. But I thank You now for the waiting periods of my life because the perseverance is producing character in me (Rom. 5:4). Holy Spirit, please strengthen me as I wait. And Lord, thank You that You are waiting to be gracious to me and that You exalt Yourself to show me mercy. In Jesus' name I pray. Amen.

77 *For the Soul That Needs Reviving*

PSALM 19:7

The law of the Lord is perfect,
reviving the soul;
the testimony of the Lord is sure,
making wise the simple.

I f you feel the need for your soul to be revived, or if you're longing for joy, or if you realize you're lacking wisdom, or if you're on a search for satisfaction, Psalm 19 is full of tender mercy for you, as it reveals that the Word of God offers all these blessings and more. Sweeter than honey and more to be desired than gold, the Bible is an undeniable demonstration of God's desire to have a relationship with us through Jesus who said, "Man shall not live by bread alone, but by every word that comes from the mouth of God" (Matt. 4:4).

The Bible's message transcends time because of its divine origin: "All Scripture is breathed out by God and profitable for teaching, for reproof, for correction, and for training in righteousness" (2 Tim. 3:16).

It's a living Book, so it will never lose its relevance: "The word of God is living and active, sharper than any two-edged sword, piercing to the division of soul and of spirit, of joints and of marrow, and discerning the thoughts and intentions of the heart" (Heb. 4:12–13).

God's Word will accomplish His purposes. Jesus said, "Do not think that I have come to abolish the Law or the Prophets; I have not come to abolish them but to fulfill them. For truly, I say to you, until heaven and earth pass away, not an iota, not a dot, will pass from the Law until all is accomplished" (Matt. 5:17–18).

Written by approximately forty different human authors over the span of fifteen hundred years, it is completely unified in its central storyline because those authors were inspired by the Holy Spirit, such that God is ultimately the Author of Holy Scripture. If you want to know God's will, it's found in God's Word. If you want to know the way to salvation, the pathway is illuminated by God's Word. "The sacred writings . . . are able to make you wise for salvation through faith in Christ Jesus" (2 Tim. 3:15).

All of Scripture points us to the Savior, Jesus (John 5:39). The Old Testament shows us our need for a Savior and foretells the coming of the Christ to save. The Gospels (Matthew, Mark, Luke, and John) tell of Jesus' birth and His life, death, and resurrection. The Acts of the Apostles tell of all He continued to do after His ascension, through sending the Holy Spirit. The epistles display His glory and teach us how to live in the light of the glory of Christ. The book of Revelation shows Him as the Risen Lamb who reigns supreme as sovereign over all and who will return for His own. The Bible is so infinitely valuable because it leads its readers and its hearers directly to Jesus, the way, the truth, and the life (John 14:6). Feast your soul on the Word of God and you will discover the riches within!

Reflect

How can the Word of God revive your soul, give you wisdom, and fill you with joy? Do you approach the Scriptures with that kind of anticipation? If not, what can you do to grow in that type of eagerness as you read your Bible?

Let's Pray

Lord, I thank You that Your Word is perfect, reviving the soul. I need my soul revived right now. Please open my eyes to see and behold wonderful things in the Scriptures, so that it has a reviving effect in my life. I pray for wisdom from above, joy and delight, refreshment and recovery, goodness and grace. Help me see the glory of God in and through the Word of God. In Jesus' name I pray. Amen.

78 *Over the Raging of the Sea*

PSALM 93:4

Mightier than the thunders of many waters,
mightier than the waves of the sea,
the Lord on high is mighty!

There's nothing on earth quite like the ocean. There's something majestic about the power of ocean tides, the relentless rhythm of its actions. It can make you jeer with laughter one moment and then knock the breath right out of your lungs as it pulls you off your feet the next. Its waves can invigorate you, and then frighten you, and then revive you again. The ocean is unpredictable. It's magnificent; it's mighty. Every trip to the beach reminds me of how the psalmist described the Lord in the verse above: mightier than the thundering of waters, stronger than the swelling waves.

Our glorious God holds the world in His hands and everything, including the ocean, is under His sovereign rule and control. When forces of evil and darkness rise and roar, threaten oppression, oppose the kingdom of God, and *appear* to rule, we must remember that God rules over the raging of the sea. It may seem like chaos is the only order of the day, that the seas are pounding with relentless abandon, and like we cannot get our footing against all that opposes us and knocks us down. But the Lord is *mightier* than the thunder of the great waters and the breakers of the sea. He controls even the crashing of the ocean tides. As the forces of evil and opposition lift their voice to roar, to wreak havoc, to terrorize, and to oppress, they are not the final authority. They are not ultimately in control. "*Mightier*" is the Lord; "The Lord on high is mighty" and He speaks comfort to His people who are tempted to fear.

But now thus says the LORD,
he who created you . . .
"Fear not, for I have redeemed you;
    I have called you by name, you are mine.
When you pass through the waters, I will be with you;
    and through the rivers, they shall not overwhelm you . . .
For I am the LORD your God,
    the Holy One of Israel, your Savior . . .
you are precious in my eyes,
    and honored, and I love you." (Isa. 43:1–4)

No matter how high the waves rise, our God is in complete control of them. My soul, trust today in your majestic, mighty, sovereign, reigning God and be refreshed again in the ocean of His love and mercy. He is almighty, and He is for you in Christ.

Reflect

Have you ever been afraid of the waves of the sea? How does it encourage you to know that God is mightier than the thunders of many waters and the waves of the sea?

Let's Pray

Father, You are in complete control of the waves of the ocean and You are in complete control of the waves of my life. You are mightier than the thunders of many waters, mightier than the waves of the sea, and Almighty over all. I look to You and trust in You today. In Jesus' Almighty name I pray. Amen.

79 · When We Can't Trace God's Hand

"Fear not, little flock, for it is your Father's good pleasure to give you the kingdom."

During trying circumstances, it can feel as if this world is falling apart around us. Rather than giving in to the despair that so easily accompanies life's difficulties, large and small, Jesus encourages us to not be anxious but to consider how God feeds the birds, clothes the grass, and provides for His children. God takes pleasure in taking care of us.

The prophet Habakkuk faced extremely challenging circumstances during a time marked by moral and spiritual corruption, political unrest, futility, and fear. At the beginning of the brief book of Habakkuk, the prophet is questioning God and is full of complaint (Hab. 1:1–4; 1:12–2:1). The Lord speaks (1:5–11; 2:2–20). Habakkuk realizes that God's justice is beyond comprehension, and that He works all things for His glory and the good of His people. So he responds with a life-altering decision: he decides that, though he doesn't fully understand everything God is up to, he is still going to trust Him through it all.

In a beautiful display of faith in God's sovereign control, infinite wisdom, and perfect love, Habakkuk pens these words of mercy and grace:

> Though the fig tree should not blossom, nor fruit be on the vines,
> the produce of the olive fail and the fields yield no food,
> the flock be cut off from the fold and there be no herd in the stalls,
> yet I will rejoice in the LORD;
> I will take joy in the God of my salvation. (Hab. 3:17–18)

Dearest believer, sometimes the fig trees of our lives blossom, the vines are full of grapes, the olive crop is rich with color, the fields produce great grain, and the sheep and cattle are abundant. At other times, our hard work is met with failure and futility as the fields produce no food. But always, the Lord of all is in control of it all. You may not be able to rejoice in *what* you're experiencing, but you can always rejoice *in the Lord* even as Habakkuk says here, "yet I will rejoice in the LORD; I will take joy in the God of my salvation."

God takes pleasure in giving His children the kingdom. We can trust His heart, even when we can't outline His hand or understand His plan. He loves us and He is for us. These simple lines came to me one day and they have often been a great source of strength, reminding me of the presence of the Lord in my life:

Take heart, my soul, and fears take flight!
God works in you to please His sight.
There's nothing to fret and nothing to fear
As long as God, my God, is near.

Reflect

Have you ever been in the place where you have been called to trust God's heart when you can't understand His plan? Are you in that place right now? If so, how does this meditation comfort you?

Let's Pray

Father, thank You for taking pleasure in giving Your children the kingdom! Lord, when it seems like things are going awry, I know I can still rejoice in You and have joy in Your salvation. So I trust Your heart even when I can't trace Your hand. I love You and I praise You. In Jesus' name, amen.

80 *Looking Up*

I lift up my eyes to the hills.
From where does my help come?
My help comes from the LORD,
who made heaven and earth.

O believer, lift your eyes heavenward! How often is your gaze *fixed* on things below! You will not find the hope you are looking for by contemplating yourself, your surroundings, or your circumstances. You need help *from above*, and you have that here in this glorious truth: "My help comes from the LORD, who made heaven and earth."

What greater help could you receive than the help from the One who made you, who made all of creation around you, who owns every morsel of land, who governs the flight patterns of the birds as they glide their way over the waves of the ocean, and who fashioned and rules over the heavenly beings, the moon, the stars, and every planet, including the earth you live and breathe on? The Lord has said, "Seek the things that are above, where Christ is, seated at the right hand of God. Set your minds on things that are above, not on things that are on earth. For you have died, and your life is hidden with Christ in God. When Christ who is your life appears, then you also will appear with him in glory" (Col. 3:1-4).

We lift our eyes not just to the hills but to the Maker of those hills, the heavens, and the earth. We fix our gaze on You, O Lord. It's incredible to think that our help comes from the Creator God. The author of Hebrews writes, "Be content with what you have, for he has said, 'I will never leave you nor forsake you.'" So we can confidently say, "*The Lord is my helper; I will not fear; what can man do to me?*" (Heb. 13:5-6). What tender mercy this is that the Lord of heaven and earth would stoop to be our helper! And yet, that is exactly what we have—help from God above: "Behold, God is my helper; the Lord is the upholder of my life" (Ps. 54:4). We are kept safe by God Himself: "The LORD will keep your going out and your coming in from this time forth and forevermore" (Ps. 121:8).

So we say, "Now to him who is able to keep you from stumbling and to present you blameless before the presence of his glory with great joy, to the only God, our Savior, through Jesus Christ our Lord, be glory, majesty, dominion, and authority, before all time and now and forever. Amen" (Jude 24–25).

Reflect

Where do you normally look when you need help?

Let's Pray

Lord, I need Your help, and I look to You for help. I acknowledge my weakness, frailty, fears, and failures. What I need is the faithfulness of the living, mighty God, Creator God. My help comes from You who made heaven and earth. Thank you for Almighty support; in Jesus' name, amen.

81 *When You Don't Know What to Do*

"O our God . . . we are powerless against this great horde that is coming against us. We do not know what to do, but our eyes are on you."

A t times, believers find themselves in a place where they are completely distraught, totally dismayed, utterly powerless, and burdened beyond their own strength. This was certainly the case with Jehoshaphat, king of Judah, when the armies of the Moabites and Ammonites and Meunites gathered against him for battle. Perhaps this is how *you* feel right now. If so, learn from Jehoshaphat's prayer.

Notice, he had no *plan*: "We do not know what to do." He also had no *power*: "For we are powerless against this great horde." What he did have was *prayer*, the willingness to express dependent faith and trust in the sovereign, all-powerful King of the universe.

> And Jehoshaphat stood in the assembly of Judah and Jerusalem, in the house of the LORD, before the new court, and said, "O LORD, God of our fathers, are you not God in heaven? You rule over all the kingdoms of the nations. In your hand are power and might, so that none is able to withstand you. . . . Our eyes are on you." (2 Chron. 20:5–6; 12)

Though Jehoshaphat was king of Judah, He conveyed reliance on the King of the universe. That's what we're to do when we don't know what to do: we lift our eyes heavenward to the One who can help us in our distress.

When our eyes are on our enemies, we will be dismayed and full of fear. When our eyes are on ourselves, we will be discouraged, and we'll lose heart. But, when our eyes are on the God of heaven, we will be assured of His help and will receive His strength, so the king of Judah says, "Our eyes are on you."

So, too, the psalmist says, "I lift up my eyes to the hills. From where does my help come? My help comes from the LORD, who made heaven and earth" (Ps. 121:1–2).

As Jehoshaphat lifted his eyes to the God of heaven, he was marvelously helped. It's worth reading the story in 2 Chronicles 20. His enemies were routed, and he was rescued by divine deliverance. Our God saves, and He offers us the same gracious invitation in the midst of our distresses, no matter their severity: "Call upon me in the day of trouble; I will deliver you, and you shall glorify me" (Ps. 50:15). Let us remember that all who are in Christ have already been rescued from our greatest distress (eternity separated from God), and if God did not spare His own Son, but gave Him up for us all, how will He not also, along with Him, graciously give us all things (Rom. 8:32)? When we're in trouble, let us follow Jehoshaphat's example and make this simple but powerful plea to the God of heaven: "We do not know what to do, but our eyes are on you." As we receive His help, may we give Him all the glory!

Reflect

Where do your eyes naturally tend to focus when you don't know what to do? How is this meditation instructive to you, encouraging for you, and comforting to you?

Let's Pray

Father, right now I lift my eyes to You. You are the Author and the Perfecter of my faith. You said, "Call to me in the day of trouble; I will deliver you, and you shall glorify me." So I take all my troubles to You, my Mighty God [share your troubles in detail]. *Please deliver me, and I will give You all the glory. In Jesus' mighty name I pray. Amen.*

82 *The Origin of All Ministry*

2 CORINTHIANS 4:1

Therefore, having this ministry by the mercy of God, we do not lose heart.

It's all too common to lose heart at times, to grow weary, to become calloused, to cultivate cynicism, and to finally want to just give up entirely.

Ministry is hard because loving others is hard, preferring others is hard, and serving others is hard, particularly when met with criticism and hostility as the apostle Paul experienced in Corinth. The natural inclination to opposition is retaliation or retreat. The supernatural response to opposition is a steadfast display of tenderness in the face of anger. This is highlighted for us in 1 Peter 2:19–24, where the apostle Peter shows us that it is a gracious thing to endure sorrows while suffering unjustly. Jesus experienced the agony of doing good and being met with oppression and torment as a response. He is our Savior and our chief example. When He was reviled, He did not revile in return, but entrusted Himself to the Father above. We are called to follow in His footsteps.

How do we *not* lose heart when others contest us for our acts of love? We remember that the origin of all ministry is mercy. Christ did good and suffered in response, in our place, as our substitute, and as our perfect example that we might follow in His footsteps. Now He pronounces blessings on those who extend His mercy:

"Blessed are the merciful, for they shall receive mercy.

Blessed are the pure in heart, for they shall see God.

Blessed are the peacemakers, for they shall be called sons of God.

Blessed are those who are persecuted for righteousness' sake, for theirs is the kingdom of heaven.

Blessed are you when others revile you and persecute you and utter all kinds of evil against you falsely on my account. Rejoice and be glad, for your reward is great in heaven, for so they persecuted the prophets who were before you." (Matt. 5:7–12)

Mercy is the origin of our ministry, it is the manner of our ministry, and it is the message of our ministry because it's the nature of the Lord: "Gracious is the LORD, and righteous; our God is merciful" (Ps. 116:5). As we have received mercy, may we also be a reflection of mercy!

Reflect

When have you been tempted to lose heart in your ministry or service to others? How does this meditation help strengthen you?

Let's Pray

Jesus, thank You for saying that we are blessed when reviled and persecuted, for great is our reward in heaven. Thank You for Your example of doing good and suffering in response, in our place, as our substitute and as our perfect example, that we might follow in Your footsteps. I'm not looking for persecution or trials, but I'm so grateful to know that when they come my way as a result of righteousness, You see, You know, and You reward. Please strengthen me by the Holy Spirit and be glorified in my life, I pray. In Your name, amen.

83 *Don't Be Surprised*

JOSHUA 1:9

"Have I not commanded you? Be strong and courageous. Do not be frightened, and do not be dismayed, for the LORD your God is with you wherever you go."

If anyone tells you following Jesus will make all your problems disappear, don't believe them. That thinking only leads to disillusionment and despair because it's simply not true. In contrast, Jesus says, "In the world you will have tribulation. But take heart; I have overcome the world" (John 16:33). Here we have grace and truth. The truth is that on this side of heaven, life is hard and those following in the footsteps of Jesus are destined for afflictions (1 Thess. 3:3). The grace is that Jesus has overcome the world, and we have infinite hope in Him.

That's why the apostle Peter writes, "Beloved, *do not be surprised* at the fiery trial when it comes upon you to test you, as though something strange were happening to you. But rejoice insofar as you share Christ's sufferings, that you may also rejoice and be glad when his glory is revealed" (1 Peter 4:12–13). Life in this fallen world is often draining and discouraging, but our God is "the God of endurance and encouragement" (Rom. 15:5). Amid all the brokenness, the Lord's tender mercy strengthens and sustains us. He speaks and quiets our fears. He lifts our spirits. He delivers us from the depths of our discouragements. He gives us peace, and He fills our hearts with hope.

During an extended season in my life that was marked by discouragement, inwardly I was cast down, though other people may not have perceived it outwardly. I was sad, burdened, lonely, and struggling hard for joy. I felt like a complete failure and wondered if God could or would ever use me again, when I stumbled upon the first chapter of Joshua and read this account of God commissioning Joshua to lead the Israelites into the promised land just after the death of Moses. God even commands the people to not be afraid, but to be strong. Courageous. How could they not be frightened? Because He Himself would be with them.

Here we have a gracious command and a precious promise. It was as if the Lord had gently but firmly grabbed ahold of my shoulders, looked me square in the eye, and said, "I know what you are going through, and I am commanding you now to be strong and courageous and to not give in to discouragement and despair." That's the gracious command. God could have ended the sentence after giving this gracious command, but He didn't. In His kindness, He also provided a precious promise powerful enough to deliver us from deep discouragements and despair: "The LORD your God is with you wherever you go."

Believer, God is with you. If you are in Christ, the God of all endurance and encouragement is with you *right where you are, wherever you go,* He is with you to sustain you, support you, and empower you. Look to Him and be strengthened by the assurance of His presence.

Reflect

What's your typical response when you encounter trials? Are you surprised by trials? How does this meditation prepare you for trouble and strengthen you during trials?

Let's Pray

Father, You have commanded me to be strong and courageous, to not be frightened, and to not be dismayed, promising that You are with me wherever I go. Thank You for this gracious command and wonderful promise. Help me now to stand strong and to not give in to fear or disillusionment, but to trust You fully. If You are with me and for me, who can be against me? I trust in You. In Jesus' name, amen.

84   *The Warmth of the Sun*

PSALM 19:1, 4C-6

The heavens declare the glory of God,
and the sky above proclaims his handiwork . . .
In them he has set a tent for the sun,
which comes out like a bridegroom leaving his chamber,
and, like a strong man, runs its course with joy.
Its rising is from the end of the heavens,
and its circuit to the end of them,
and there is nothing hidden from its heat.

There is something about gazing up at the beauty of God's creation amid its habitual daily rhythm of renewal that speaks so strongly of the glory and faithfulness of God. Every morning as the sun rises, the steadfast love of the Lord is on display, and every evening as the sky fills the horizon with radiant colors in the brilliance of the setting sun, God welcomes us to commune with Him.

To breathe in the crisp evening air, to view the pattern of birds in their twilight flight, and to pause long enough to watch this magnificent star lower her head below the horizon soothes the spirit and has a calming and restorative effect upon the soul. Every single morning and every single evening, the goodness of our tenderly merciful God is on display in the activity of the sun. Whenever you feel the warmth of its rays, let it remind you of the warmth of God's love.

The sun should draw our attention to the Son. "He is the image of the invisible God, the firstborn of all creation. For by him all things were created, in heaven and on earth, visible and invisible, whether thrones or dominions or rulers or authorities—all things were created through him and for him. And he is before all things, and in him all things hold together . . . that in everything he might be preeminent" (Col. 1:15–18).

As nothing is hidden from the sun's heat, so no one is outside of God's affectionate reach. So daily we are reminded by God that He is preserving and governing His creation in total faithfulness. Day after day the skies pour forth speech, and night after night they display the knowledge of God (Ps. 19:2). Let's step outside and gaze and gape and marvel in wonder at the glory of God's love on display in the sun and through the Son. When the expectations of our workdays come to a close, may our hearts lift heavenward and find the peace, rest, quiet tranquility, and communion with the living God we inwardly crave. "The LORD is good to all, and his mercy is over all that he has made" (Ps. 145:9). Let's pause in prayerful awe and grateful praise and let the warmth of God's love fill us with wonder anew.

Reflect

What's the best sunrise you can ever remember seeing? What's the best sunset? Where were you, and what emotions did it evoke? How does this meditation draw your attention to the glory of God?

Let's Pray

Father, thank You for putting Your goodness and mercy on display every morning, every afternoon, and every evening in the activity of the sun. Whenever I feel the warmth of its rays, please remind me of the warmth of Your great love. Help me be more and more mindful of Your glory every moment of every day. In Jesus' name I pray. Amen.

85 *How God Never Feels*

Have you not known? Have you not heard?
The LORD is the everlasting God,
the Creator of the ends of the earth.
He does not faint or grow weary;
his understanding is unsearchable.

Whenever you feel weary and fainthearted, remember this simple thought and it can help you turn your weariness into worship: *God never feels this way.* Incredible. The Lord is the everlasting God, and the Creator of the ends of the earth is infinite in His power and wisdom. Our hearts will soar heavenward when we allow *our* weakness to remind us of *His* strength.

Your exhaustion is an opportunity to worship the everlasting God. Let this thought sink in and amaze you: God doesn't grow tired and He never faints. He is never fatigued, and nothing can deplete His energy. So we can worship Him for His power!

Unlike God, we are not self-existent, and we are not self-sufficient. We are dependent creatures, and we rely on God's strength. The good news is that out of the storehouses of His might, the infinite, self-existent, all-powerful God mercifully gives strength to the weary: "He gives power to the faint, and to him who has no might he increases strength" (Isa. 40:29).

What a promise! Weary one, there is strength for you in the power of your all-mighty God. Weak and worn out as you are, God can make you strong. Fainthearted and fatigued believer, let your exhaustion be an occasion for exulting in the energy of God. Turn your weariness into worship and find your strength in God above: "Even youths shall faint and be weary, and young men shall fall exhausted; but they who wait for the LORD shall renew their strength; they shall mount up with wings like eagles; they shall run and not be weary; they shall walk and not faint" (Isa. 40:30–31).

Are you weary? Remember this: God is never weary. Wait upon the Lord. Renew your strength. Turn your weariness into worship and you will fly like an eagle out among the stars.

Reflect

Are you weary right now? Have you ever considered turning your weariness into worship? What would that look like?

Let's Pray

Lord God, You have inexhaustible power and strength. You're never tired and You never grow weary or fainthearted. I worship You as the everlasting God with boundless, unending vigor and might. Please steady my knees and increase my strength for Your glory. In Jesus' name I pray. Amen.

86   *The God of Hope*

*May the God of hope fill you with all joy and peace in believing,
so that by the power of the Holy Spirit you may abound in hope.*

When our attention is fixated on ourselves, we easily get discouraged. The roller coaster of our own performance is a miserable ride. On the other hand, when our focus shifts to God and all that He is for us in Christ, our souls begin to soar. So let us fix our eyes on the Lord, the founder and perfecter of our faith (Heb. 12:2).

He is the God of hope. No matter what is happening in your life right now, the God of hope wants to fill you with all joy and peace in believing, so that by the power of the Holy Spirit, you abound in hope. Believer, you died with Christ, you have been raised with Christ, your life is now hidden with Christ in God, and when Christ who is your life appears, you also will appear with Him in glory (Col. 3:3–4). What a hope you have in Jesus!

He is the God of all comfort. Second Corinthians 1:3–4 says, "Blessed be the God and Father of our Lord Jesus Christ, the Father of mercies and *God of all comfort*, who comforts us in all our affliction, so that we may be able to comfort those who are in any affliction, with the comfort with which we ourselves are comforted by God." God knows your pain, and He cares deeply for you in your struggles. As your trials come, so will your comfort. The Lord is mercifully inclined to comfort you and console you; He will not waste your pain but will redeem it all for your good and for His glory.

He is the God of endurance and encouragement. "May *the God of endurance and encouragement* grant you to live in such harmony with one another, in accord with Christ Jesus, that together you may with one voice glorify the God and Father of our Lord Jesus Christ" (Rom. 15:5–6).

God is almighty, and in His infinite power, He is able to fill you with strength and courage to continue to run the race and not give up until you see Him face to face in glory.

He is the God of peace. Romans 16:20 assures us, "*The God of peace will soon crush Satan under your feet.*" You may be surrounded by turmoil, grief, and heartache, and the enemy of your soul is actively seeking to destroy your faith. But your God is the God of peace, and the enemy will be soundly defeated. The battle wages on, but your final victory is as sure and certain as if it is already yours!

He is the God of all grace. We read in 1 Peter 5:10, "After you have suffered a little while, *the God of all grace*, who has called you to his eternal glory in Christ, will himself restore, confirm, strengthen, and establish you." Because God is the God of all grace, you can be assured that your sufferings will be followed by glory. All His grace is in store for you. You may feel broken, weak, and faltering but you will soon be restored, confirmed, strengthened, and established.

Take heart, dear believer. This is your tenderly merciful God!

Reflect

What encourages you the most about God right now—that He is the God of hope, the God of comfort, the God of endurance and encouragement, the God of peace, or the God of all grace? Why?

Let's Pray

Lord, I praise You that You are the God of all hope, the God of all comfort, the God of all endurance, the God of all encouragement, the God of all peace, and the God of all grace. I need Your hope, Your comfort, Your strength, Your peace, and Your grace. Please fill me with Your Spirit, and let my life reflect that You are my God. In Jesus' name, amen.

87 *What We Were Made For*

All things were created through him and for him.

All of life makes sense when we realize we are made through Jesus and for Jesus. We could forget everything else we have ever known, but if we "remember Jesus Christ," we know everything we ever need to know (2 Tim. 2:8). He is the One who made us, who is the founder of our faith, who is our constant provider, and who will sustain us to the end. Everything we will ever need is found in Him!

You and I were made *for Jesus*. It is easy to get so caught up in living the Christian life that we forget the Christ for whom we are living. We can easily become more aware of what we are doing for God than what God has already done for us in Christ. When we look in the mirror and focus only on ourselves and our accomplishments, we walk away either puffed up with pride or derailed by despair.

On the other hand, when we fix our eyes on Jesus, we are aligned again with our purpose and with ultimate reality. Jesus is the image of the invisible God (Col. 1:15). He is our Creator and sustainer (vv. 16–17). Ultimately, everything exists for Him (v. 16). That means that our life is more about Jesus and who He is than it is about ourselves and who we are or what we have done (or not done). Indeed, it is only when we remember Jesus that we truly remember who we really are.

Looking to Jesus, we come to grips with the reality that we are sinners, even as Simon Peter did when he realized he was in the presence of sovereign holiness: "He fell down at Jesus' knees, saying, 'Depart from me, for I am a sinful man, O Lord'" (Luke 5:8). Looking to Jesus, we realize that we could never earn God's favor or merit His love. Nevertheless, looking to Jesus, we remember He came to save sinners (1 Tim. 1:15;

Eph. 2:1–10) and all who have believed in Him are now new creations in Christ (2 Cor. 5:17).

We have been crucified with Christ, and it is no longer we who live, but Christ who lives in us. The life that we now live in the flesh, we live by faith in the Son of God who loved us and gave Himself up for us (Gal. 2:20). Though we have fallen short of the glory of God (Rom. 3:23), we have been justified by His grace as a gift, through the redemption that is in Christ Jesus (Rom. 3:24). This is amazing grace!

Reflect

Can you remember a time when you were more aware of what you were doing for God than what God has done for you in Christ? What did that look like?

Let's Pray

Lord Jesus, thank You for helping me understand what my life is all about. I was made through You and for You. Please open my eyes to see more and more of Your grandeur and Your magnificence. My life will never make sense apart from You. I humble myself and acknowledge You as my Lord and Savior. Mesmerize me with Your glory, I pray. In Your name, amen.

88 *The Secret to Contentment*

PSALM 4:7

You have put more joy in my heart
than they have when their grain and wine abound.

The believer's true joy is never circumstantial, but relational. It's a joy located in a person, not in a position or station in life. David sets his joy in God against the fleeting pleasures of those whose highest hope is worldly prosperity. In his mind, if offered the choice between all the riches of the world without the Lord, or nothing but the solace of a cold cave with Him, David would choose the latter with joy.

The psalmist directs his praise upward to the source of true joy when he proclaims that God has made him more joyful than when the harvest is plentiful and the wine "gladden[s] the heart of man" (Ps. 104:15). Christ's presence is the secret to your contentment in every circumstance. God can make great gladness surround even the sparsest of tables. He can set the crown of delight on the poorest of heads. This is a joy that outrivals the most jubilant palace of the world because it is a joy that is outside of the assaults of any enemy.

Look to Christ, and you can sing even in the most miserable of conditions. Hear Paul and Silas fill a prison with melodious sounds of upward delight just after being beaten, shackled, and bound like common criminals, and know that you, too, can have this kind of joy (Acts 16:23–25). Jesus is the fountain of all true delight; knowing Him adds loveliness to every condition and is a mercy in every affliction. If I have all the riches of the world without Jesus, I have nothing. If I have Jesus and nothing else, I have everything. He is all I need (Prov. 15:16–17).

Whom have I in heaven but you?
And there is nothing on earth that I desire besides you.
My flesh and my heart may fail,
but God is the strength of my heart and my portion forever.
For behold, those who are far from you shall perish;
you put an end to everyone who is unfaithful to you.
But for me it is good to be near God;
I have made the Lord GOD my refuge,
that I may tell of all your works. (Ps. 73:25–28)

Reflect

If offered the choice between all the riches of the world *without Christ*, or a life with nothing fancy but Christ, what would you honestly choose? Why? What does this reveal about the state of your heart?

Let's Pray

Lord, Your presence brings blessing into any situation. In Your presence is fullness of joy and at Your right hand are pleasures forevermore. Fill me with joy in You and let the world take note of how good and glorious and gracious You are, so they put their trust in You too. In Jesus' glorious name I pray. Amen.

89 *Again, Again, and Again*

PSALM 71:20-21

You who have made me see many troubles and calamities
will revive me again;
from the depths of the earth
you will bring me up again.
You will increase my greatness
and comfort me again.

Notice the word "again" in this passage. Three times the psalmist employs it here: again, again, and again. What a mercy is found in that one little word, *again*! It matters not how many times you have come, you can keep coming back to God *again, again, and again*! For the comfort you crave, for the deliverance you desire, for the revival your soul longs to receive, you can come to God for it all again, again, and again. Over and over and over, He will receive you and revive you until you reach the haven of heaven's peaceful shore. Take comfort in knowing that God will supply what you need as you need it.

Life is full of troubles and calamities, but every distress submits to the Sovereign One who rules over all. That's why the psalmist says, "*You who have made me see many troubles and calamities will revive me again.*" Even Satan had to ask permission to afflict Job, and unless God had granted it, no affliction would have been allowed to touch him (Job 1:6–12). Humbly and rightly did Job proclaim, "The LORD gave, and the LORD has taken away; blessed be the name of the LORD" (Job 1:21). The One who rules and reigns over our troubles is the One who can also relieve them.

Psalm 71 offers the hope of comfort, the hope of restoration, the hope of revival, and even the hope of resurrection.

God can resuscitate the lifeless and revive the most reviled. If it's the first time or the five millionth time, it matters not, because you can keep coming back to Him for life and renewal. He can bring you up from the depths of the earth; He can increase your greatness and comfort you *again, and again, and again*! Trust in Him and turn all your troubles over to Him . . . again . . . right now.

Reflect

Do you believe you can keep coming back to God again, again, and *again*? What comfort does it give you to hear that God will supply what you need over and over and over again? What do you need right now?

Let's Pray

Father God, thank You that I can keep coming back to You again, again, and again for the mercy I need, for the grace I need, for the comfort I need, for the strength I need. Please revive me again, bring me up from the depths again, and comfort me again for Your glory. I pray this in Jesus' trustworthy name, amen.

90   *The Reason We Persevere*

JEREMIAH 32:40–41

"I will make with them an everlasting covenant, that I will not turn away from doing good to them. And I will put the fear of me in their hearts, that they may not turn from me. I will rejoice in doing them good, and I will plant them in this land in faithfulness, with all my heart and all my soul."

The pledge God speaks of in this passage is *a covenant of grace.* This is not a conditional agreement based on our performance or grounded in our good works. God promises here *a new covenant* of grace and mercy rooted in His own everlasting love, and it is glorious in its reach. The Lord promises to *continually do us good.* He will not turn away from us. He will not forsake us. He will not stop doing good to us.

The Lord also promises here to put a holy fear of Himself in our hearts, so we will not turn away from Him. Not only will He not turn away from us, but He will incline our hearts to never turn away from Him! We will persevere until the end as He preserves our hearts for Him. The reason we persevere is because He preserves. Our perseverance is an outworking of His guarantee to keep our hearts from turning away from Him. In a beautiful passage in John 6:37–40, Jesus communicates the eternal security of His followers, saying that whoever comes to Him, He will never cast out, and that He will keep each one safe until the last day when they receive eternal life.

He later says, "My sheep hear my voice, and I know them, and they follow me. I give them eternal life, and they will never perish, and no one will snatch them out of my hand. My Father, who has given them to me, is greater than all, and no one is able to snatch them out of the Father's hand. I and the Father are one" (John 10:27–30). You can count on it.

You are safe in God's hands, forever and eternally secure!

Not only does the Lord say He will keep us, but He also says *He will take great delight in keeping us.* "I will rejoice in doing them good, and I will plant them in this land in faithfulness, with all my heart and all my soul." God does not simply tolerate His people; He celebrates us! He rejoices over us with gladness, under the covenant of grace! Let these words wash over you as a benediction:

> The LORD your God is in your midst,
>> a mighty one who will save;
> he will rejoice over you with gladness;
>> he will quiet you by his love;
> he will exult over you with loud singing. (Zeph. 3:17)

What peace, what comfort, what joy it brings to be safe and secure in God's salvation!

Reflect

Do you usually believe God is tolerating you, or celebrating you? How does this meditation encourage, comfort, or strengthen you?

Let's Pray

Father, thank You for the everlasting covenant that You have made with me in Jesus. Thank You for promising to never turn away from doing me good. Thank You for promising to continually inspire me to fear You, so that I won't turn away from You. Thank You for taking great joy in doing me good. I trust now in Your faithfulness and steadfast love. In Jesus' name I pray. Amen.

91 *Blessed to Bless*

GENESIS 12:2

"And I will bless you and make your name great, so that you will be a blessing."

Here is the divine intent behind the blessing of Abram. God purposed to prosper Abram and to make his name great as Abraham (see Gen. 17:5), *so that he would be a blessing*. Indeed, in him all the families of the earth are blessed, as Abraham is the spiritual father of those who live by faith in Christ (Gen. 12:3b): "So then, those who are of faith are blessed along with Abraham, the man of faith" (Gal. 3:9).

Proverbs affirms that "a good name is to be chosen rather than great riches, and favor is better than silver or gold" (Prov. 22:1), but the Lord gave Abraham all of it: a good name, favor, *and* great riches (Gen. 13:2). Yet none of this blessing from above was due to Abraham's own personal merit. It was solely out of God's sheer benevolent goodness and sovereign mercy. It's clear that Abraham was not a perfect man (see Gen. 12:10–20). The blessing of God was by the mercy of God, for the glory of God, and for the blessing of countless others.

Believer, the same is true for you as it was for Abraham. If you are blessed by God—if your name is made great as you experience the favor of a good reputation, or if you are entrusted with the power of increased riches, or if you experience the blessing of *both* riches and reputation—remember the divine intent.

The Lord is blessing you *so that you will be a blessing.* Stagnant waters are breeding grounds for disease and death, but a flowing brook breeds life. Just as it says in Ezekiel, "wherever the river goes, every living creature that swarms will live. . . . For this water goes there, that the waters of the sea may become fresh; so everything will live where the river goes" (Ezek. 47:9).

Blessed believers are designed as conduits of divine mercy and blessing for others. You are *blessed to be a blessing*. So go and enrich the lives of everyone around you for the glory of God above.

Reflect

Where do you believe the Lord has blessed you *so that* you will be a blessing? What could it look like for you to bless others with the blessings you've received?

Let's Pray

Father God, thank You for the way You have blessed me—with life, with breath, and with everything else You have provided for me in Your great love. Please help me take every blessing and turn it into blessing for others. Use me as a conduit of tender mercy and great grace for others in my life. I pray in Jesus' blessed name, amen.

92 *Tenderhearted*

EPHESIANS 4:32

Be kind to one another, tenderhearted, forgiving one another, as God in Christ forgave you.

God's heart for us is intended to fuel our heart for others. We're instructed to pattern our lives and conduct after His example (John 13:15; 1 Peter 1:15–16; 2:21). So it's no wonder that we are called to be kind to one another, tenderhearted, forgiving one another, as God in Christ forgave us. It's in view of the mercies of God that we offer our lives in worship to Him (Rom. 12:1–2).

What does God's mercy look like practically?

God is kind. Jesus instructs us, "Love your enemies, and do good, and lend, expecting nothing in return, and your reward will be great, and you will be sons of the Most High, for he is kind to the ungrateful and the evil. Be merciful, even as your Father is merciful" (Luke 6:35–36). My soul, hasn't the Lord been kind to you? While you were still an enemy, Christ died for you (Rom. 5:8–11). The precious blood of the Savior was the heavenly response to all your pride. What kindness is this! Soaking our souls in the kindness of the Lord is the best way to inspire us to live lives of kindness and mercy toward others.

God is tenderhearted toward you. It was the tender mercy of our God that ushered in the promised Messiah (Luke 1:78–79). Even in the midst of stubborn opposition, God's compassion grows warm and tender (Hos. 11:8c). "For he makes his sun rise on the evil and on the good, and sends rain on the just and on the unjust" (Matt. 5:45). Softhearted, gentle, sympathetic, compassionate, and benevolent is God's heart. When we meditate on His loving character, it melts our hard hearts and we want to emulate His tenderness in our dealings with others.

God forgives. "To the Lord our God belong mercy and forgiveness" (Dan. 9:9). What's incredible is that He shares His mercy so freely with us. Scripture proclaims that everyone who believes in Jesus receives forgiveness of sins through His name (Acts 10:43). In Him, "we have redemption, the forgiveness of sins" (Col. 1:14). God is kind. God is tenderhearted. God forgives when we confess our sins (1 John 1:9). This is why we're to be kind to one another, tenderhearted, forgiving one another, as God in Christ forgives us.

Reflect

When you think about God's kindness, God's tenderhearted nature, and God's forgiveness, how does that affect the way you think of people in your life?

Let's Pray

Lord God, I thank You for Your kindness. You have been so kind to me. I thank You for Your tender heart. You have been so gracious with me. I thank You for Your forgiveness. You have covered over a multitude of my sins. Please help me now, by the power of the Holy Spirit, to be kind to others, tenderhearted, forgiving others as I've been forgiven in You. In Jesus' name I pray. Amen.

93 *More than Enough*

MATTHEW 16:9-10

"Do you not yet perceive? Do you not remember the five loaves for the five thousand, and how many baskets you gathered? Or the seven loaves for the four thousand, and how many baskets you gathered?"

How quickly we can forget the mercies of God brought to us in answer to our earnest prayers! We cry out in our distress, the Lord delivers us, and then like the Israelites we forget the works He has performed on our behalf. Our hearts are prone to wander, and that wandering starts the moment we forget the wonders God has done (Ps. 106:13).

Lord, please save us from our spiritual amnesia!

God's grace and mercy have always been more than enough. Jesus and the disciples were in a boat, heading across the lake. When they reached the shore, they remembered that they hadn't brought anything to eat. Though Matthew 16:9–10 doesn't spell it out, we can assume they started to worry and fret about provisions for a meal. That's when Jesus asked, "Don't you remember . . . ?" God is able to fully satisfy the multitudes with a plentiful provision. Just as the disciples picked up leftovers after the miraculous meals the Savior provided, so God meets our needs such that we have room to share as our cup runs over (Ps. 23:5).

So let's not forget, whether it's a work God did for us yesterday or a year ago.

I will remember the deeds of the LORD;
  yes, I will remember your wonders of old.
I will ponder all your work,
  and meditate on your mighty deeds.

Your way, O God, is holy.

What god is great like our God?

You are the God who works wonders;

you have made known your might among the peoples.

You with your arm redeemed your people. (Ps. 77:11–15)

Remember and do not forget the deeds of the Lord, the wonders He has done, and all His works on your behalf. And when you remember, lift your soul in songs of praise that His mercy and His grace have and will always prove to be more than enough for you!

Reflect

What mercies in your life do you tend to forget, and what mercies do you need to continually call to mind and remember forever? How can you keep from forgetting those mercies?

Let's Pray

Father, I'm so prone to wander from You, and I'm so prone to forget Your goodness and the great things You've done in my life. Please forgive my wandering and forgetful spirit, and please take my heart and seal it for Your courts above. In Jesus' name I pray. Amen.

94 The Lord Is Near

PSALM 145:18-20

The LORD is near to all who call on him,
to all who call on him in truth.
He fulfills the desire of those who fear him;
he also hears their cry and saves them.
The LORD preserves all who love him.

Just as any *human* relationship is built through regular communication, so our relationship with God is strengthened as we daily interact with Him. We experience God's nearness the more we call on Him: "The LORD is near to all who call on him, to all who call on him in truth." Prayer (calling on God) and prayerful meditation on the Word of God (calling on God *in truth*) are our chief means of experiencing the tenderness and nearness of God.

Some people may feel pestered by constant contact, but this is not the case with the Lord. God wants to hear your voice, and the more often, the better!

Jesus tells a story about someone coming to a friend at midnight and asking for three loaves of bread to feed a guest who arrived at his house. His friend said, "Do not bother me; the door is now shut, and my children are with me in bed. I cannot get up and give you anything."

Jesus continues the story. He explained that the man finally got up and gave his friend what he had asked for. But he didn't do so out of friendship; he did it because of the friend's persistence. Jesus said we too should be persistent. "Ask, and it will be given to you; seek, and you will find; knock, and it will be opened to you. For everyone who asks receives, and the one who seeks finds, and to the one who knocks it will be opened" (Luke 11:5–10).

Jesus tells this story to encourage us to pray with boldness continually. The more we call on the Lord, the closer we will sense His presence. "But for me it is good to be near God; I have made the Lord GOD my refuge, that I may tell of all your works" (Ps. 73:28).

Communion with God takes place when we take the real mess of everyday life directly to the real God for real grace. When we do this, the Lord draws near (James 4:8), we sense His nearness, He hears our cries, He responds to our pleas, and He preserves and fulfills our desires for His glory. Let Him hear what you need. Give Him the opportunity to hear your cries, fulfill your desires, and grant deliverance in response to your requests.

The Lord is near to all who call on Him and the nearness of God is our highest good!

Reflect

What *real mess* of your everyday life do you need to take directly to the *real God* for *real grace*? Talk to Him about it now.

Let's Pray

Father, thank You that You are not irritated by my voice. You're not bothered by my constant need. You welcome my cries. That's amazing grace. So here I am again, coming to You this day with the real mess of my life. Please help me with everything I'm going through [tell Him what you're struggling with]. *I put all my trust in You. In Jesus' name I pray. Amen.*

95 *Mercy Unrestrained*

PSALM 40:11

As for you, O LORD, you will not restrain
your mercy from me;
your steadfast love and your faithfulness will
ever preserve me!

S ome picture the Lord as impatient, touchy, and ready to pounce on every hint of defiance, but that is not the true heart of God. The deepest heart of God is full of compassion and tenderness toward His creation, even toward those who resist His influence and spurn His holiness.

God's heart is to restrain His anger and to generously pour out His mercy. "For my name's sake *I defer my anger*; for the sake of my praise *I restrain it for you*" (Isa. 48:9). Picture the righteous anger of God being held back with greater power than the Hoover Dam, while the mercy of God is more unrestrained than the might of Niagara Falls.

The truth is God is not like us who are irritable, easily infuriated, and ready to fight back. The Lord is long-suffering, patient, and compassionately forgiving. Hear this gracious plea:

Seek the LORD while he may be found;
   call upon him while he is near;
let the wicked forsake his way,
   and the unrighteous man his thoughts;
let him return to the LORD, that he may have compassion on him,
   and to our God, *for he will abundantly pardon.*
For my thoughts are not your thoughts,
   neither are your ways my ways, declares the LORD.
For as the heavens are higher than the earth,
   so are my ways higher than your ways
   and my thoughts than your thoughts. (Isa. 55:6–9)

God is so patient with us, not wishing that *anyone* would perish, but all would come to life in Him (2 Peter 3:9). He says He has *no pleasure* in the death of the wicked but yearns that the wicked would turn from his way and live (Ezek. 33:11). The Lord desires that all people would be saved and come to a knowledge of His truth (1 Tim. 2:4). God in compassion remembers that we are but flesh, and He restrains His wrath (Ps. 78:38–40).

God's kindness should have a softening effect on our own hearts, as it is meant to lead us back to Him in repentance and faith (Rom. 2:4). Repeatedly, the Scriptures portray the Lord as "merciful and gracious, slow to anger, and abounding in steadfast love" (Ex. 34:6; Pss. 86:15; 103:8).

Daniel could no sooner begin his appeals for mercy than be met with reassurance of steadfast love from above (Dan. 9:23), and the same will be true for you! God is rich and generous with His mercy (Eph. 2:4), and He will be rich and generous with His mercy toward *you*. Call out to Him in faith, and He will compassionately meet you with *mercy unrestrained*.

Reflect

How does picturing the Hoover Dam and Niagara Falls help you understand the way God restrains His anger and pours out His mercy?

Let's Pray

Father, thank You that You are so eager to pour out Your mercy on me, that I can say, "As for you, O Lord, You will not restrain Your mercy from me; Your steadfast love and Your faithfulness will ever preserve me." Thank You that I'm living under unrestrained mercy. Let Your mercy fall over me like a waterfall, and help me bask in the wonder of Your steadfast love and faithfulness. In Jesus' name, amen.

96 *Return*

2 CHRONICLES 30:9B

"For the LORD your God is gracious and merciful and will not turn away his face from you, if you return to him."

The prodigal son knew he had made a complete mess of his life after he had wastefully squandered his entire inheritance in reckless living; he had nothing left to live on when a famine arose in the country. So he hired himself out to a pig farmer, but even the pigs were fed better than he was. In the depths of his despair, he decided to humble himself and return to his father's house and beg for the job of a hired servant, feeling himself unworthy to even be called his father's son.

Incredibly, instead of encountering the harsh judgment or reluctant reception he imagined, this wayward-yet-returning son was overwhelmed with a gracious and merciful welcome from the very father he had scorned. As he was still a long way off, his father saw him and was filled with compassion, and he ran to his son, embraced him, kissed him, clothed him with the finest robe he had, put a ring on his finger and shoes on his feet, and threw him the most epic welcome party with the finest of foods! Dear reader, if you feel far off from the Lord, this story is meant for you. God wants you to know that you will have the same reception from your Father in heaven when you return to Him.

Just as this father received his wayward son with great delight, so too, the Lord your God will receive you with joy as you return to Him. Backsliding, straying one, wait no longer; return to your heavenly Father and you will receive anew His grace and mercy as He celebrates over you: "I tell you, there will be more joy in heaven over one sinner who repents than over ninety-nine righteous persons who need no repentance" (Luke 15:7). The Lord your God is gracious and merciful.

Reflect

Can you, in any way, relate to the prodigal son in this passage? If so, how does this meditation comfort your soul? What will you do in response?

Let's Pray

Father, I'm so amazed at Your kindness; You welcome me and any who have drifted from You to return to You, no matter how far we have strayed. And instead of meeting us with condemnation and judgment, You overwhelm us with mercy and favor. Lord, I return to You completely. Thank You for receiving me. I'm Yours completely. In Jesus' name, amen.

97   *The God of Unshakable Peace*

ISAIAH 54:10

"For the mountains may depart
and the hills be removed,
but my steadfast love shall not depart from you,
and my covenant of peace shall not be removed,"
says the LORD, who has compassion on you.

God's love for us is stronger and higher and fiercer than the tallest of mountains. Mount Everest would appear like an ant hill compared to the vastness of God's steadfast love. The Lord has eternally and unwaveringly set His affection on His children, and His compassion will forever remain. This earth will pass away (Matt. 24:35), but His Word will stand firmer than Mount Kilimanjaro.

Believer, you are under a covenant of unshakable peace, and it shall not be removed from you because the Lord has compassion on you. "Since we have been justified by faith, we have peace with God through our Lord Jesus Christ" (Rom. 5:1). The peace we have is a permanent peace, not one that can be altered in any way. Our redemption is eternally secure (Heb. 9:12c). Every continent would sink into the bottom of the world's oceans before God would remove His steadfast love from you or take away His covenant of peace. Take heart, trembling one, your future is incredibly bright and eternally secure in Christ.

I love the confidence of the apostle Paul as he writes, "I am sure of this, that he who began a good work in you will bring it to completion at the day of Jesus Christ" (Phil. 1:6). The work God started in you will continue and continue and continue until it is fully and finally completed. If you have experienced any bit of the mercy of God, you shall receive all of it. Jesus said, "For I have come down from heaven, not to do my own will but the will of him who sent me. And this is the will of him who sent me, that I should lose nothing of all that he has given me, but raise it up on the last day. For this is the will of my Father, that everyone who looks on the Son and believes in him should have eternal life, and I will raise him up on the last day" (John 6:38–40).

Our God is compassionate, gracious, merciful, and all-powerful, and He will forever hold you firm in His faithful, steadfast love!

"Now may the God of peace himself sanctify you completely, and may your whole spirit and soul and body be kept blameless at the coming of our Lord Jesus Christ. He who calls you is faithful; he will surely do it" (1 Thess. 5:23–24).

Reflect

What's the most strenuous hike you've ever taken, or the tallest mountain you've ever climbed? How does it encourage and comfort you to know that God's steadfast love and His covenant of peace are mightier than the mountains?

Let's Pray

Father, thank You for Your ceaseless compassion and Your promise of peace. You melt my heart with Your mercy. Please use me for Your glory, even as I hide myself in You. In Jesus' compassionate name I pray, amen.

98 *The Door of Mercy*

PROVERBS 28:13

Whoever conceals his transgressions will not prosper,
but he who confesses and forsakes them will obtain mercy.

W e've meditated considerably in this work on the mercy of God. Yet as we approach our final pages, perhaps I am speaking now to one who still feels like a foreigner to the gift of mercy. If you, dear reader, still feel "far off" there is great hope for you in our present text. Here is a special combination to unlocking the door of mercy, and you are invited to try this code. It has worked for myriads of sinners over thousands of years, and I believe it will work for you as well.

There are two paths laid out for us in this passage. The first path is that of *contempt*. The second is that of *confession*. In this meditation, let's consider each in turn.

The path of contempt will never even lead a seeker to the door of mercy, let alone be able to unlock it. It's a false path of pretense and insincerity and those who pursue it will not prosper. Jesus illustrated this cleverly in Luke 18:9–14. He told a parable to some who trusted in themselves that they were righteous and treated others with disdain: "Two men went up into the temple to pray, one a Pharisee and the other a tax collector. The Pharisee, standing by himself, prayed thus: 'God, I thank you that I am not like other men, extortioners, unjust, adulterers, or even like this tax collector. I fast twice a week; I give tithes of all that I get.'" This is the path of contempt, and Jesus shows that this individual did not prosper.

The path of confession, on the other hand, delivers the seeker directly to the door of mercy. It's then that the combination code can be used for entry. Here's the code: confess your sins, your need for a Savior, and your trust in the Savior, then forsake your transgressions, turn away from them and turn to the Lord in faith, and the door of God's mercy will fling wide open! This is the door the tax collector took, and He received mercy:

> "The tax collector, standing far off, would not even lift up his eyes to heaven, but beat his breast, saying, 'God, be merciful to me, a sinner!' I tell you, this man went down to his house justified, rather than the other. For everyone who exalts himself will be humbled, but the one who humbles himself will be exalted." (Luke 18:13–14)

If you confess your sins, turn away from your sins, and turn in faith to the Savior, you, too, will be saved. Everyone who trusts in Jesus receives mercy from above, and God bestows His riches on all who call on Him (see Rom. 10:9–13; John 3:16–17).

Which path will you choose?

Reflect

When you consider the path of concealment and the path of confession, which path have you been on recently? Which path would you like to be on? How then will you respond?

Let's Pray

Lord, You have promised to extend mercy to those who confess and forsake their sins. So I'm done hiding. Here's what's really going on [confess it all]. Please cleanse me, forgive me, and fill me with the Holy Spirit as I turn away from my wrongdoings and turn in faith to You. I pray in Jesus' name, amen.

99 *All Things New*

PSALM 23:4

Even though I walk through the valley of the shadow of death,
I will fear no evil, for you are with me; your rod and your staff,
they comfort me.

The worst thing that can happen to us in this world—death—
simply delivers the believer from this mortal body to put on
immortality in everlasting joy. We can be confident, even as we walk
through the valley of the shadow of death, because God is with us, and
He will never leave us nor forsake us (Heb. 13:5–6).

You who are in Christ have a hope that is secure beyond the grave,
because you have a Savior who has conquered death by His grace. Jesus
is alive (Luke 24:5–6). He has defeated death and, by His resurrection,
He has secured for us eternal life. So, believer, you have an inheritance
that can never perish, spoil, or fade, kept in heaven for you who by God's
power are being guarded, sustained, and preserved through faith for a
salvation that is ready to be revealed (1 Peter 1:4–5).

Revelation 21:1–7 anticipates the fulfillment of the heavenly vision:

> Then I saw a new heaven and a new earth, for the first heaven
> and the first earth had passed away, and the sea was no more.
> And I saw the holy city, new Jerusalem, coming down out of
> heaven from God, prepared as a bride adorned for her husband.
> And I heard a loud voice from the throne saying, "Behold, the
> dwelling place of God is with man. He will dwell with them,
> and they will be his people, and God himself will be with them
> as their God. He will wipe away every tear from their eyes, and

death shall be no more, neither shall there be mourning, nor crying, nor pain anymore, for the former things have passed away."

And he who was seated on the throne said, "Behold, I am making all things new." Also he said, "Write this down, for these words are trustworthy and true." And he said to me, "It is done! I am the Alpha and the Omega, the beginning and the end. To the thirsty I will give from the spring of the water of life without payment. The one who conquers will have this heritage, and I will be his God and he will be my son."

O death, where is your victory?
O death, where is your sting? (1 Cor. 15:55).

Reflect

When you think of death, what emotions surface in your heart? How does this meditation comfort you as you consider the inevitability of dying?

Let's Pray

Lord Jesus, You have conquered death. You died, and three days later You rose from the grave. Now You have ascended to the right hand of the Father, and You ever live to make intercession for Your own. Thank You for the hope I have in You—a hope that extends beyond this life and beyond the grave, which You defeated. Please strengthen me even when I walk through the valley of the shadow of death. May Your perfect love cast out all fear. In Your precious name I pray. Amen.

100 *Multiplied*

JUDE 1-2

---

*To those who are called, beloved in God the Father and kept for
Jesus Christ: May mercy, peace, and love be multiplied to you.*

We conclude this devotional with a personal prayer for every reader. "May mercy, peace, and love be multiplied to you." God knows your heart and your history; He knows the pains and the pleasures of your life; He understands the highs and the lows, the ups and the downs, the twists and the turns of this ridiculously wonderful thing we call life. He meets you exactly where you are and has grace and mercy available for your every need. May the Lord Himself strengthen you and establish you and multiply His mercy, peace, and love to you.

For every reader:

"May the God of hope fill you with all joy and peace in believing, so that by the power of the Holy Spirit you may abound in hope" (Rom. 15:13).

"May the Lord direct your hearts to the love of God and to the steadfastness of Christ" (2 Thess. 3:5).

"May the Lord of peace himself give you peace at all times in every way. The Lord be with you all" (2 Thess. 3:16).

"For this reason I bow my knees before the Father, from whom every family in heaven and on earth is named, that according to the riches of his glory he may grant you to be strengthened with power through his Spirit in your inner being, so that Christ may dwell in your hearts through faith—that you, being rooted and grounded in love, may have strength to comprehend with all the saints what is the breadth and length and height and depth, and to know the love of Christ that surpasses knowledge, that you may be filled with all the fullness of God.

Now to him who is able to do far more abundantly than all that we ask or think, according to the power at work within us, to him be glory in the church and in Christ Jesus throughout all generations, forever and ever. Amen" (Eph. 3:14–21).

"To him who loves us and has freed us from our sins by his blood and made us a kingdom, priests to his God and Father, to him be glory and dominion forever and ever. Amen" (Rev. 1:5–6).

"The grace of the Lord Jesus be with all. Amen" (Rev. 22:21).

Reflect

Of the prayers in this meditation, which resonate with you the most? What is your deepest desire as you conclude this devotional? Tell it to the Lord.

Let's Pray

Father God, thank You that You know my heart and my history, all the pain and the pleasures of my life, the highs and the lows, the ups and the downs, the twists and the turns, the challenges and the joys. And You promise to meet me exactly where I am with grace and mercy for every need. You are so good, so gracious, so generous, and so glorious. My life is Yours. In Jesus' name, amen.

Acknowledgments

I would like to sincerely thank everyone who offered personal encouragement, counsel, comfort, and strength as I wrote *Overflowing Mercies*. Numerous friends continuously expressed their excitement about this work, and many have prayed that this book would be blessed by God to serve those who read it. To all of you who have privately offered support, *thank you* (if you're wondering if that's you, it is!).

To my readers: whenever you invest your resources to purchase a book or your time to read something someone has written, *you* offer your support for the author's work. I want to sincerely thank everyone who has picked up a copy, left a positive review, and shared this devotional with others. I am so grateful to God for you.

My wife, Laura, is my biggest ally. Thank you, Love, for encouraging me to keep writing (though it often represents sacrifice on your part). Thank you for reading every word, for providing helpful and hopeful feedback, for reassuring me when I'm disheartened, and for walking with me through every step of this writing process and this unpredictable life. I love you with all my heart.

To the team at Moody Publishers, it's such an honor to work with you to advance the gospel and to strengthen the church for the glory of Jesus! I want to specifically thank my acquisitions director, Trillia Newbell, for championing this project and for your steadfast friendship over the last three decades. Thank you to my publisher, coworker, and dear friend, Randall Payleitner, for adding this title to the list of Moody books. Thank you to Pam Pugh for your outstanding editorial skills and cheerful attitude—it's such a pleasure working with you!

Thank You, Lord, for Your love because every ounce of *Overflowing Mercies* comes from above. Please bless this book for Your glory.

An unlikely friendship shows how God works
in the everyday lives of those who love Him.

100 MEDITATIONS ROOTED IN GOD'S WISDOM AND FAITHFULNESS

To become wise, we must respond to Wisdom's call—to dwell in Wisdom's house. K. A. Ellis shows us how to claim the asset of wisdom and invites us to experience Jesus Christ—the Wisdom on which our world rests. Ellis calls us to live as people who are *wise*.

Also available as an eBook and audiobook

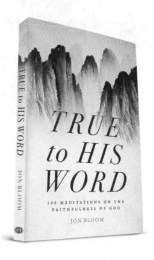

Is there healing for the heartaches and setbacks in life? Are there promises we can hold on to—Someone who won't let us down? Jon Bloom ushers us into a journey into the character and faithfulness of our triune God. We can praise and trust God even in dark seasons.

Also available as an eBook

MOODY
Publishers®

From the Word to Life®